Journey of a Running Girl

By Kristina Clay

Journey of a Running Girl

Kristina Clay

Copyright © 2025 by Kristina Clay

All rights reserved. No part of this book may be reproduced, stored in a retrieval system, or transmitted in any form or by any means—electronic, mechanical, photocopy, recording, or otherwise—without prior written permission from the publisher, except for brief quotations in reviews or articles.

ISBN: 979-8-218-64740-7

For permissions, inquiries, and bulk orders, contact: :
tina.clay@1icloud.com

To my young self, who survived when it seemed impossible.

To my family, who showed me what unconditional love feels like.

And to God, for guiding me through every dark street into the light.

TABLE OF CONTENTS

Prologue 1
Chapter 1 Silently Crying For Help 37
Chapter 2 Leaving Everything Behind Forever 61
Chapter 3 Blending In 71
Chapter 4 Being Able To Tive and Not Exist 87
Chapter 5 Summer Camp as an Orphan 97
Chapter 6 The American Christmas 109
Chapter 7 Third Time Is A Charm 127
Chapter 8 Goodbyes 143
Chapter 9 Time To Go 169
Chapter 10 The American High School Experience ... 179
Chapter 11 Memory Of The Dead 201
Chapter 12 The College Graduate 205
Epilogue 223
Acknowlegements 225

PROLOGUE

This book is everything that I am today. Literally. No holding back, not even a little bit... If you ever thought about knowing me, the true side of me - this is it. With all honesty and after reading this book you'll probably agree with me that if it weren't for Kevin and Aileen Clay, I wouldn't even be here today. This book wouldn't be here today.

I'd be another lost cause, another "poor" girl without parents, but oh well, because where I come from, everyone has a story. Everyone has something to say about their life based on their life choices and their looks. Because where I'm from, even people's eyes talk and have a beginning and an end.

But that's not me - thanks to Kevin and Aileen, my story is different because the main difference between me and those other "poor lost causes" is that society has labeled them based on their parents' choices, based on where they were born into and importantly what kind of family there were born into. Where I'm from, you can't just walk away because, believe it or not, it's not THAT simple. But the main difference between me and all those poor children left behind is that I have the opportunity to be heard. I have the power, and it is my voice. The power to tell you my story and the story of other children who are now forgotten and don't matter because it's their fault that they were born into a poor family in a small village somewhere in the middle of Europe. Because it's their fault that from the second they were brought onto this earth, their whole life has already been decided for them. Step by step.

This book is everything I am today, and I am truly blessed for the life lessons I've been through because now it's all part of me and everything that I am today. Thank you all for believing in me and not giving up. I owe a thank you to my parents, my siblings, my boyfriend Emilio for dealing with my mood swings while writing this, and my high school teachers who saw potential in me before I did myself.

CHAPTER 1.
THE BEGINNING OF THE CHILDHOOD ERA

All my life, I've been running, running away, to be more specific. Running away from my grandparents, school, friends, and even myself sometimes. Everything. Just so I wouldn't have to face the reality of who my family was. Who I was turning into because of my family. One moment, my whole life fell apart, and I genuinely thought that no super glue could ever glue me back together.

That is how I ended my running journey in the states, across the Atlantic Ocean. I want to be heard. I want to tell you my story from my perspective and how I felt in the shittest situations. My goal is to make a difference and give hope to children who were faced with the same challenges as I was growing up and still do. So, stay with me.

My name is Kristina. I have been called Kristina by my family members and friends for a good fourteen years of my life. After I got adopted, Kevin and Aileen told me that I could choose a nickname that was somehow associated with my legal name, like Kris. I hated the way Americans pronounce my name, I still do. It was really rare to hear someone say my name and roll the "R" like my friends and I do. I hated the fact that Americans spelled my name with a ch and not k. Now, everywhere I go, like picking up my monthly prescription at Walgreens, and the lady behind the counter asks my name, I have to either spell my name out or let her know that my name starts with a k and not ch.

Because if I don't, they going to tell me that I am not in the system.

When I was given the opportunity to start over and even have a new name, I would be stupid not to take it. I didn't even have to think hard enough about it; without hesitation, I looked into my parents' eyes and proudly announced that from that moment, "I would like to be called Tina". They smiled and didn't ask any questions; instead, they said they could make that work. The reason why I said I wanted to be called Tina is because, in Ukraine, we have a somewhat related family member. I had an uncle who died from alcohol poisoning when I was a little girl. He wasn't my biological uncle or even a great uncle, but somehow, we were related. He had a sister, and his sister's best friend was my aunt's best friend; her name was Natasha. She lived so far away from us, yet once in a few years when, either my aunt or grandfather were drinking out of their mind, they undecidedly just decide to show up on her doorstep with a bottle of Vodka in their hands. She never turned us down, and she never said no to Vodka. She was absolutely drop-dead gorgeous, and I 100% think my grandfather had a crush on her for the longest time. Whenever we'd visit Natasha, and she would see me coming out of the vehicle or crowd, she would rush towards me, pick me up and scream with love in her voice, "Tinka". Tinka is the soft version of Tina, and she was the only person in Ukraine who had ever called me that. Being called Tina definitely gave me the power to have a different personality when I was around Natasha, and I absolutely loved it.

Since I was always on the move, I was blessed with the opportunity to meet lots of various kinds of people. When I sensed some sort of trust from that person, I would share my story and explain why it was so messed up. They would listen with open mouths and tell me that I have unique life experiences and that I have been blessed. I'm not going to lie; it does feel sometimes that I am special in some ways. I often ask myself why me? Why me out of millions of other children who also suffered and silently cried for help. Who were and still are in need of a family. A family that could remind them what it is like to be loved. Yet, out of all of the orphanages in the country, out of all the cities, out of all broken children - it was me. Why?

The most unexpected things happen to those who aren't looking or waiting. However, I did wait. I waited longer than I should've. I don't believe in magic, yet some Godmother or Fairy Tale was sent my way - to open up my eyes and pinch my arm so I would wake up from a dream that was never happening. To wake me up and show me that no one I cared about was coming to get me. To save me from all the mess I got myself into because of my family. I was all sort of messed up, so they got rid of me. I knew that I was not the easiest child to handle. At some point down the road, when I realized that no one was coming back for me, I made myself accept it and move on. I had people who took me out of the pile of dirt and helped me to find purpose. Everything is different.

It doesn't matter if it is a good or bad difference because it is still better than it used to be.

Close your eyes and try to remember your childhood days as vividly and clearly as possible. Are your memories full of laughs with your happy family? Is it a memory of crying because you fell and scratched your knee while trying to learn how to ride a bicycle? But your parents were there to pick you up and tell you, "It's okay honey", as they would blow on your boo-boos. Is it a memory of a family vacation in the Bahamas creating the PERFECT memories with your PERFECT family? Is it a memory of your parents sharing the news that you're going to have a younger brother or a sister? Or… Is it you crying? Constantly crying…not knowing what life has for you because you felt worthless? Questioning what your next meal is going to be or where you're going to spend the night? Question yourself: Whose fault is it that both of your parents walked away from you? Finding no other answer and ending up blaming yourself for everything because it seemed the easiest to do? If that's what comes to your mind, you are not alone because I can relate. The childhood that I had was the worst that you could imagine. I didn't have any surprise birthday parties, no cute puppies, no family vacations, or iPhones for Christmas. Let me give you a virtual tour of the only home I ever knew before the age of 12. The home I was taken away from. The home that caused forever scars.

From the outside, all one could see was four walls built from mud, two windows, a roof, and a front door. But then that is all you really need to have a normal house, am I right?! My grandfather always tried to add fancy things to make our home look homie on the inside; he knew that people judged us based on how poor we looked with our mud walls. Mud would fall off the walls whenever it rained, and every spring, you would see my grandmother on her knees trying to fix the holes in our walls; you can imagine that our walls were not straight, not on the outside nor inside the house. By taking out a TV loan, fancy vacuum loan or a fancy microwave loan from the banks, he tried to make our home look somewhat modern and normal. Every time we had visitors who weren't ashamed to come inside, either my grandfather's drinking buddies or child support, they were always impressed with how our house looked on the inside.

My whole house has only two rooms. In the summer, we left our shoes outside before entering the house. There was barely enough space for everyone to breathe, and keeping everyone's shoes inside would just add more chaos. As you'd come inside, there was about half a foot drop, and the floors were always cool even though we had rugs over it. Right to the left was a ladder leading to the attic, where we could store our junk, but that's about it. To the side of the ladder against the wall, a few hooks were drilled into the wall to keep our jackets hanging. Under the ladder, however, we had a bucket that we would use as a bathroom, and yes, I know what you're thinking; we all heard each other's business. The bucket would get covered and emptied into a hole my grandfather had dug just for that purpose.

The hole he threatened to bury me in if I won't stop disobeying him, but even my future grave didn't scare or even stop me from running away from this family. In the summer, we were able to use the outside bathroom, which was pretty much a porta potty but also with a bucket, and after taking out the bucket, it was used as a summer shower. Straight ahead, we had a few tables against the wall, and on those tables, we were able to cook, prep, and eat sunflower seeds while either gossiping or watching intense drama TV shows, and of course, where I used to do homework. On top of one of those tables, we had an electric stove, where most of the time, the spirals were working or jammed or only working 50%. The spirals my grandfather was too afraid to fix, the spirals that my grandmother had to fix on her own, and the spirals that we were too broke to fix. On the third table, we had a TV; on the other side of the room was a bed against the other wall. This was the bed where my grandmother slept; this was the bed where I sometimes slept with my grandmother, where I spent most of the nights falling asleep on her chest while she played with my hair or massaged my arm.

This is where I slept with my grandmother when I was sick, and I couldn't sleep in the other room because my cough was keeping my grandfather up. This was the bed where my grandmother slept because, yes, my grandparents slept alone, in separate beds, in separate rooms. Just a few feet above the bed, there was a giant piece of wood drilled into the wall, serving our family as a shelf. A shelf that was covered with some cheap material was where my grandmother was able to keep medications along with her makeup, foundation, and one red lipstick that burned when it touched your lips because of how old it was. The only times when she wore foundation were real few, when we had to go to a few towns over to school shop or do my yearly doctor check-in for school.

Under the bed space was serving us as storage, where we could keep boxes of green tomatoes and some onions. Once the chilly weather arrived, we were able to use fresh homegrown tomatoes in late fall. Vegetables like tomatoes, cucumbers, carrots and so on weren't sold at the grocery stores because this is something people grew in their gardens. Once the season was over, it meant no fresh vegetables until the next season. In late fall, we were able to keep some pears and apples, but those didn't last long because instead of eating one apple a day like a normal child, I would eat about five at a time and go to bed with a stomachache. Behind the bed, last thing there was a door, a door that opened to another room, a door that was always opened and closed when I was getting my ass whipped by my grandfather. He kept the door locked so I wouldn't run out. There were times when I bit him and took off for days. The second room treats us as "my bedroom", a living room, and my grandfather's bedroom. As you'd step into the second room to the right, you'd notice an empty corner. The whole floor was covered with a rug, and some parts of the room were even double rugged to make it look richer, I guess?! Yet, that empty corner was not covered with a rug; instead, it had linoleum but not the fancy version that you have in mind.

THE BEGINNING OF THE CHILDHOOD ERA

And that corner I will never forget. Whenever I was getting punished, my grandfather would put me into that corner and make me stand on my knees with my back and knees straight as the linoleum was covered with salt. I had to spend hours and sometimes the whole night on my knees, holding a pillow with my arms in the air. To worsen my punishment, sometimes I had to hold two little bottles filled with water in each hand with my hands straight. Doing so, I had to face the wall; I would stare into nothingness as I silently cried, and if I had my arms down just for a slight second or if they weren't straight, my grandfather's voice would hunt me from the other side of the room "Arms straight".

Sometimes, during the night, I would fall asleep without even noticing and wake up the next day on the couch; the salt would get glued to my knees, making them bleed. Yet, my grandfather wasn't the kind to forgive for pity, and once the nighttime came again, without even guilt in his eyes or voice, he would say "do it again". During the summer, I had to do this lovely exercise by standing on wood outside, and instead of bloody knees, I had splinters. Whenever someone came over and saw me in such a position, the word spread fast. That corner in the second room of the house still brings tears to my eyes.

Next to the corner was a table pressed against the window where we would eat lunches and dinners together on the days when no one was fighting. And let me tell you, those days were rare. Next to that table, there was a chair pressed against the wall; above that chair, we had a picture hanging of Mother Maria holding Jesus Christ. Not knowing if God existed, I asked Mother Maria for so many forgivenesses. I asked for favors too. I would say, "God, if you exist, please make my mother love me again," and that's also where I prayed for my grandparents to give me a baby goat, how silly of me. Next to the chair was a folded couch that served me as my bed at night. Whenever my aunt was visiting us, she would sleep with me on that couch, and we would spend the whole night cuddling.

On that exact couch, I asked my grandparents if I could call them "mom" and "Dad", because I was getting tired of being called orphan at school. I was getting tired of being that kid with no parents. But my request was denied. My grandmother, with tears going down her cheeks, told me that even though my mother abandoned me, she still existed, even though on paper, my mother wasn't actually my mother, she still existed. Next to the couch, there was a small but tall dresser that was my closet; with about five small shelves, I almost had something that belonged to me. Pressed against the dresser, there she was, my school desk with all her glory. Though the school desk was pressed against the dresser, it was sticking out to the center of the room. You can imagine how many corners of the dresser I have kicked, on accident, of course. It was filled with a bunch of school crap that was always a mess, where my box and notebooks would fall out and I would get yelled at for being gross and not having my school desk cleaned. Next to the dresser, there was a big closet, the closet that belonged to my grandparents. Since the closet had no doors but open shelves, my grandmother had to put a fancy enough material over it, so strangers wouldn't look at her clothes. Right pressed against that closet, there was my grandfather's bed, a queen bed I shall add; it was bigger than my grandmother's and, more importantly, the comfiest. On the other side of the bed, there was a shelf, again made out of a giant piece of wood; this way, we were able to have another TV, and just like that, my house tour came to an end.

This is where my grandfather watched his news, after which he would scream in my face, "look at the news: another child being killed at the orphanage, and if you won't stop making the decision you have been making, you'll end up at the orphanage too." And not going to lie; after every conversation I had with my grandfather, well, I wouldn't call that a conversation because I wasn't allowed to speak. Every time my grandfather would bring another child being killed or just brought to the orphanage, I would silently mimic him. And deep down, I think he knew I wasn't taking him seriously because I thought that it could never be me. I thought I was so smart and could outsmart just about anyone, and the thing is, I really did. I survived just doing so for longer than I should have. And after seeing my friends being taken away by the child support system, you would think that I would've learned my lesson... yet not quite. I just learned how to be smarter and how to run quicker.

Before my grandfather took out another TV loan from the bank, this was how we awkwardly watched TV together as a "family"— my grandfather and I would lie on his fancy bed, and my grandmother would be at my school desk. Whenever she would cook some sunflower seeds and I was laying in my grandfather's bed, I was not allowed to eat sunflower seeds or anything else. And, if we ate it at my school desk, we would get yelled at for chewing too loudly to loud. For sunflower seeds make a noise, and even for having a single sunflower seed shell on the ground afterwards. So, we learned a lesson not to eat sunflower seeds while watching something with my grandfather.

After a two-hour movie ended, my grandmother would usually say that her back was killing her, and it was time or her to lay down. Ouch, a phrase such as "I'm going to lay down" was pretty much banned in my house; if my grandfather heard those words come out of my grandmother's mouth, he would then give her a speech on how lazy she is and even bring up the fact that she doesn't do anything in the house outside of the chores that she is always supposed to DO as a wife. So, my grandmother learned to avoid that phrase around my grandfather, and instead, she would say, "Good movie" or "Nice, bye". Yet even then, my grandfather still had the balls to "assume" that she was going to *lay down* after spending two hours sitting on a wooden chair that was most definitely crooked. Meaning, yes, he spent the whole movie laying in his cozy bed. Unending nights full of screaming, physical and mental abuse, non-stop drinking, and more. That's what my childhood was like.

(In the photo: Tina's grandparents' home from the street view. Photo was taken on November 23rd, 2022).

THE BEGINNING OF THE CHILDHOOD ERA

(In the photo: Tina's grandfather Vladimir. Photo was taken on November 23rd, 2022)

My childhood was full of so much darkness that all the good from it disappeared or was forgotten. Mostly because the "good" was only temporary in our family. Meanwhile, there was always a reason or a person why the "bad" turned into permanent. Like a devil who kept sucking the so little happiness that my family had created and cherished in little moments such as a holiday or another drunk night. I had to fight for myself because there were days when people I thought would never leave me just walked away from me or gave up.

Now, this isn't a childhood I dreamed of or asked for, but I dealt with it. I believe that everything happens for a reason, and if God gave me this type of lifestyle, at the end of the day, I truly hoped that something powerful and magical would happen to me. As a young girl, I got to live life as if it was a survival test. I got so wrapped up in it that

I didn't get a chance to see the world around me. Important to see the good in people, that not everyone around me is going to cause pain and leave me all over again. No one taught me any different, so I grew up thinking I was all alone, thinking that at the end of the day, no one had my back but myself. I never got to live in the type of world that a normal teenager lived in. At the end of the day, I was never the "normal teenager". Being happy and enjoying my youth was definitely not on the list of the girls who tried to survive.

From the very start, I thought that I was the problem. I thought I was a curse that made my family fall apart. Yet, the worst part about it is that not a single person around me made me think otherwise. I always thought my life got messed up since the day my biological father, Vitaly, walked away from my mom and me. I never met my biological father. I only have a memory of him from a picture that my aunt showed me once. I ended up burning the picture afterwards. Seeing my mother with some stranger who carried the title of my father made me angrier and angrier as I stared into the stranger's eyes. Without any hesitation, I just ripped the picture down the middle. I'm not sure if, at that point, I was hurt or jealous or all of the above. I was desperate for my mother's attention. Damn, I was desperate for my father's attention too! I wanted to be wanted, a I wanted to be wanted, to be a complete family once in my life. Seeing them together made me feel that my mother was everywhere but not with me.

The picture was the only time I saw my father, and from what I remember, he was tall, young, and stupid. He was stupid for leaving my mom and me. Growing up, I always thought my biological parents left me because they didn't want me or weren't ready for a child. I always thought that I was a mistake and was born at the wrong time. My

THE BEGINNING OF THE CHILDHOOD ERA

family did nothing, absolutely nothing to make me feel I belonged. I was never a center of attention around my family; whenever we had people over, and I tried to be a part of a conversation, I would get told to get lost and find something better to do. So, I would do what I was told: get lost. I would run away; then I was the dumb one because I took it too seriously....

It took me years to realize that I am who I am today because of me and no one else. My goal is to never turn into the kind of people my family were. It took me years to realize that I was born not because I was a mistake but because I was meant to be born. I deserved to be alive.

Ever since I was born, I told myself I never had a childhood. Because that is exactly how it felt, and even to this day, I still stand by that because I don't remember being happy; what I do remember is being scared to come home to face my grandfather. I remember being scared. I remember being cold and hungry. I remember seeing tears. I remember hearing furniture break and hearing screams of the loved ones that caused my body to cringe and cause infinite pain. All I did was run away, get beat up, get myself into trouble and hide, and the next day, the cycle would repeat. I saw things in my life that a six year old girl should never have seen. There are some things that I wish I could unsee and forget. Unfortunately, life doesn't work that way. There were days I wished that it would've been someone else, literally anyone, just not me.

I was told that the moment my biological mom, Olga, found out that she was pregnant with me, she was really excited to share that news with Vitaly. Sadly, he didn't feel the way Olga did. He ran away, saying that he wasn't ready to be a father yet, that he was too young and wanted to live a normal life - whatever that meant.

I was born On February 26th, at 10:00 am, in Nikopol, Ukraine, or at least that's what I thought my whole life. And let me tell you, living about two years without a father wasn't bad at all. That's because I don't remember all the real struggles my mom faced to make sure I had shelter, food in my stomach, and a smile on my face as a single mother.

I remember stories my aunt used to tell me, such as how my mom would feed me ramen soup to the point where I wouldn't be able to go to the bathroom for days. Soon or later, her parenting days came to an end, and looking back at it now, I wonder if I was just an experiment for her. I mean, who just does that? Who has a child, keeps it around for a little bit, and then just decides that parenting isn't it and leaves? Mothers who have the nerve to walk away from their children and pretend to be innocent and that it is okay, should see a therapist. At some point, she couldn't do it all. I can't write from her perspective because I don't know her side of the story and why she left me, but I know 100% that she gave up on me. I also know that if I asked her why she did it, she wouldn't be able to give me an okay enough answer for me to forgive her. I was two and a half years old when my mom came to the conclusion that she was too tired of being a mother. She had this overwhelming feeling of loneliness, and I was too needy. I guess it was my fault for not being an independent woman at the age of two and a half.

I was told she didn't even have the balls to drop me off safely at my grandparent's house. Instead, she asked our neighbor girls to walk me to see my grandparents, Nadia and Vladimir, with a note in my pocket. Now, you are wondering what the note said, and before you get any ideas, no, it was not a suicide note. The note said something like, "Can Kristina stay with you for a little while? I want to find Vitaly."

THE BEGINNING OF THE CHILDHOOD ERA

Even though it had been a couple of years since he left her, she still loved him. I am pretty sure he was her first love. She thought she loved him until she found out the real reason why Vitaly left her. During the time when Vitaly and Olga were just dating, Vitaly was already married to a woman with whom he had seven children. She got played. You would've thought that after running into a dead-end, she would've turned around to be with her family, to be with me. At that moment, she was on the edge of the cliff in life, ready to jump off. She started to drink excessively to the point where she would eventually become an alcoholic. Who knew that my staying at my grandparents' house "for a little while" would turn into many years.

One summer, my grandfather's brother showed up. I never knew he had a brother before?! Neither did anyone else in our family. Maybe it was one of those cases where my grandfather considered his friend as a "brother", and he never was blood-related? That is still a question that no one knows an answer to. When this so-called brother just showed up at our house, so many questions were raised, like how did he know where we lived? How come NO ONE knew about his existence??? I don't remember his name, and it's not even that important, but what was important was how fake he was. He showed up unwelcome, as far as I know, trying to impress everyone about this "brotherhood" that he and my grandfather shared. I'm not going to lie; my grandfather did seem really happy at the moment, but not for long. After half a day of drinking, they all decided to go to the lake for a picnic. As a young girl at the time and at that moment, I had so much fun being in a car full of drunk people trying their hardest not to swerve as much. There were about seven people in a four-seater car, and most of them were trying to give the driver directions at the same time. Chaos. It's crazy looking back on it and how much danger they all put me through. But I don't remember being scared. I remember just laughing my ass off because they all looked so silly. I remember being happy for a slight moment because, for a minute. I valued that with all of my heart.

Once we finally parked at the lake, that's when the party started. My aunt's friends who lived down the street from the lake came, and people just kept showing up. Even my friends came. I didn't invite them. They just showed up unintentionally, but it was good timing. Occasionally, when no one was looking, my aunt would give me a sip of her beer. It felt dangerous.

Hours later is when shit went down. Of course, no one was surprised, but I was upset. Upset that we couldn't even have a solid day where no one was arguing with anybody. But I guess when there's alcohol involved, it's impossible, especially with my family. They were the magnet to trouble. Wherever they went, it followed them everywhere, and I guess I now understand who and where I got that from. The fight was between my grandfather's "brother" and my aunt. The "brother" decided to get sexually involved with my aunt's friend.

My aunt didn't care who her friend slept with. What she did care about is the fact how drunk she was. She couldn't walk straight, and she was losing her balance and leaning on people, and instead of talking, she mumbled. What pissed my aunt off the most was the fact that he didn't care about any of that. He took advantage of my aunt's friend because he knew she wouldn't be able to say no. Within seconds, my aunt grabbed an empty beer bottle and started swinging at my grandfather's "brother." I was scared. I wasn't scared for my aunt. I was more scared for the guy she was swinging at. Because I knew she was a savage. She didn't care that the guy was almost four times bigger than her or that he was taller. She didn't care that she didn't know him, where he came from, or if he had any connection. Soon enough, before the swinging turned into a fist fight, my grandfather managed to calm my aunt down. It was obvious that the party was over... It felt wrong getting into his car after what had just happened. With no questions asked, the "brother" and his buddy got into his car and drove off very aggressively. So, we walked home, the walk was about 30-40 minutes, and since we were taking our sweet time, it was most definitely more than 40 minutes.

At the time, we didn't think about anything; we were all processing what had just happened. We started asking my grandfather how he knew his buddy whom he proudly calls "brother." He tried his hardest to change the topic. He didn't want to talk about it in my presence. But my aunt didn't want to leave it alone. It's hard enough to change her mind or mindset when sober, but under the influence of alcohol it's a whole other level. It's either her way or the highway, pretty much. Grandfather not answering us and mumbling something under his nose made the whole situation more awkward than it already was. It looked like he was hiding something, something huge, something that he was ashamed of. It made sense why he felt the way he did. He tried to hide away from me, and most importantly, because he didn't want me to be afraid of him. He didn't want me to think he was a monster, and the funny thing is, I already thought he was a monster... He tried to hide away the fact that he went to jail. I'm not sure when and why, but that's how he met his brother. It makes sense why they had the same tattoos. It's always the tiny details.

Once we got home, the "brother" was not at the house. Neither was his buddy, it felt good to know that the drama was over and no one was getting their butt kicked. At least not today, but in our family, I wouldn't be surprised if that would take a turn real fast. My grandfather's mood was the first thing that took a turn approximately five minutes after we got home. He had anger in his eyes. He kept screaming something about a knife being missing. A knife that his grandfather gave him after he graduated from the military. That knife wasn't just any knife. Besides being an incredibly special item that had been in his family for generations, it was also a dagger with someone's signature on it. The only person in our family who had a phone was my aunt. We didn't have his phone number, nor did we know where he lived, so everything was pointless. Calling the police was a waste of time. They would have just laughed in our faces and would have demanded money for nothing from them. I was scared. I left the shed for my own good after I saw my grandfather throwing glass plates and mugs against the walls. I have seen him act like this before, and people in America would label him with anger issues. It's like you aren't allowed to feel without being labeled with something.

Growing up, I always had some type of label attached to me. From the second I was born, I was already carrying the label of being fatherless. When my mother walked away from me, and my grandmother became my legal guardian at that point, I was labeled as an orphan. Then I was that girl who didn't have friends or that girl who only hung out with hooligans. At the shelter, I was that girl who didn't have hair or looked like a boy. At the orphanage, I was that girl who owned only one pair of pants. In America, I was that girl who got adopted and that girl who was from overseas. I was always something. It's like a sickness or a disease I couldn't get rid of.

Staying with my grandparents was both the worst and best years of my life. If my mother had never given up on me, I would have never known what a true feeling it is to have a strong bond with your grandparents. Yet, I also wouldn't know how it is to live with alcoholics. More importantly the feeling of the broom breaking on my back. I would have never gotten the chance to see the true side of a man - how powerful they can be and how mistreating a woman was something they were capable of, no matter their age.

THE BEGINNING OF THE CHILDHOOD ERA

(Village Velikaya Znamenka, School #3).

Dear Mother,

I am no longer sure if you deserve to be called a mother. You never were one, and just because you gave birth, doesn't mean you are one. If you ever decide that you want to be in my life, the closest thing you can ever be is a friend. That's it. I don't have a lot to offer you, and I genuinely don't want anything from you in return because I know that you would even suck at being a friend. But if you genuinely wanted to be a part of my life, you would've done something about it. I guess I still have high expectations.

Before I got adopted, I hated you. Literally, all the good memories were gone because my heart was full of hate. I mean, we don't even have good memories?! You always left me for something more expensive, shinier, for an older guy; I mean, should I keep going? Although, as I am growing up, I am starting to realize why you did what you did. I want to understand you. I want to hope that after ignoring all the shit you ever put on me, all the problems you caused in my life that somewhere deep down, you are still somewhat a decent person. You had your reasons. You were a young, beautiful lady - and I was too needy. I get that. Yet, it is not my fault you were a selfish bitch who abandoned me. Just so you could live your life up and do whatever the fuck you want, you found sleeping with men who were twice your age more important than your child. It is all on you. I do not think that you ever just sat down and thought of me, or any of your life choices, or the fact that you lost me and possibly won't ever see me again. I don't love you. You don't deserve my love. You did only what was good for YOU, what would benefit YOU, what would make YOU happy.

What about my happiness? You put me through hell. I had to live the life I lived because you weren't there for me when I needed you the most. When I needed you to talk about the simplest things. You weren't the one who made me breakfast before school, and you weren't the one who asked me, "How was school today?" Whenever you'd visit us, I would slightly hope that maybe one day you'd stay and never leave me again. Yet, every time you came to visit - you'd leave like it was nothing. Like I meant nothing to you. You don't know how I felt! So, let me tell you. I was the happiest girl whenever you'd visit. I wanted the whole town to know that you were visiting ME. That I finally had a woman by my side that I could proudly call my mom. I thought you were my happiness - but I thought it wrong, and that's my fault for being too naive. You have no idea what it is like to have the title "Orphan." You have no idea what it is like to carry the freak title because I lived with my grandparents. Whenever you had to leave, it felt like a piece of me would go with you, and at some point, there was no longer a happy girl. You did nothing to call yourself a mother because you know nothing about being one. You failed. It may be selfish of me to say this, but I blame everything that happened to me on you. If you didn't reject me, if you let me be a part of your life - I would've never known what it's like to be an orphan."

She was never there. My mother, I mean. For the most part, she could fit under the definition of a stranger because at times, that's how I felt about her. My biological mom wasn't there for me when I said my first words, or when I stated first grade at the age of six, She never showed up on my class picture days, and she wasn't there when I learned how to count from one to ten, and she wasn't even the one who taught me math, or the one who taught me literature. She never helped me practice my multiplication tables, and she wasn't there when I began to summarize poems in the fifth grad.

My aunt and my grandmother were the ones who had to step up and be there for me every time I got sick. Every time I would run away or would get myself into trouble. I go to class meetings, go to school shops with me, teach myself how to cook, and even hand wash my clothes. I got made fun of because I didn't have a Mom or a Dad. Like officially on the piece of paper because my mother was still alive and my father?! He did exist at some point in my life.

When I had "parents' meetings" at school, my grandmother would go instead of my mom. My classmates would call me names, point fingers at me, and scream "orphan" in my face. Whenever we had doctors come to our school for a checkup, they would make each grade line up with our health file in our hands. My classmates would turn around to point at me, and almost everyone would smirk because, with big fat letters, my file had "Orphan" written. Doctors would always pay a little closer attention to me whenever I was getting checked because I was an orphan and anything that looked suspicious was worth writing down. The nurse would make comments about my shirt, that it needed to be washed because it had food stains all over it. Comments about the dirt under my nails. Comments about my hair not being perfectly brushed. Anything. They would keep digging and digging and digging in front of all of my classmates.

When I was in second grade, we got a letter from my mom. This was the first letter that she sent me since I saw her last. Before that, there weren't any birthday cards, any "I'm okay", or "I love you, Mom" letters. In the letter, she talked about all her boyfriends and how she wasn't regretting anything or any of her decisions. This meant she didn't miss me, she didn't care about me, and she didn't want me, so she got rid of me. Even though the letter didn't say that, that's exactly how I felt. That was the day when I found out that my biological Dad overdosed on heroin. When I tell my story to others, they tend to flip the switch and feel bad for me. It's like they are trying to take my pain, many nights of crying, and the suffering away. The problem is that there is no pain. There is no suffering. Yet, there are scars and an ugly childhood full of unforgettable memories.

When people are trying to have a conversation with me about my biological father, I stay quiet. Not because I don't feel comfortable talking about him but because I have nothing to say. How could I possibly talk about a person I've never met or seen in my life? I could've built an image of my father in my head and lived by it?! Yet, that's too much effort for just a stranger. My grandparents kept him on the low by not talking about him when I was around. I heard them talking badly about him because he left me, he left me, so I had to grow up without a father. I don't blame him. He had a choice to make, even if it wasn't the right one. I don't hate him, I feel bad for him. I feel bad for him because he never got a chance to meet me, to see who I've become after he abandoned me after he had sex with my mom and just walked away from us. He was a drug addict, but he had no right to end his life the way he did. He had a whole family of his own that needed him. Dolgov Vitaly. When I say my father's full name, I feel nothing—no goosebumps, no pain, no memories, just an emptiness that cannot be filled in.

Growing up without parents in Ukraine is actually really common. I wouldn't be as pissed as I am right now and have been for so many years if Olga would just leave me alone. I would've been so much better not knowing half of the shit that I did. Because everything she did made me assume that she would rather be somewhere else, love someone else, and live with someone else. That someone else who was never me. Yet, the fact that she was so close to me and would just show up unannounced made me feel worthless. Every little visit of hers was like a scar or a reminder that she is doing so much better without me. I hate her. I would rather live and not know that she was sleeping with half the town for some 20 Ukrainians that wouldn't even get her far. I hated the fact that for one of my birthdays, she gave me a half-working bike and a bottle of wine, and she really thought that it would make up for all of the other past birthdays that she never showed up to or simply called to wish me a dumb happy birthday. It takes absolutely no effort to dial a number and stay on the line until the person you are trying to reach picks up the phone.

IT LITERALLY TAKES NO FUCKING EFFORT. Yes, I am angry. I am angry that women like Olga have no problem with getting pregnant and giving birth. Meanwhile, there are so many healthy, beautiful women who try to have a baby and cannot. I am angry that she gets to live a happily ever life; meanwhile, almost fifteen years of my life went to shit because of a decision she made years ago. I am angry that now I have to live with trust issues because a woman who gave me birth walked away from me as if I was a stranger. I am angry because she made me think I didn't matter, and for the longest time, I really thought I had no life purpose and told myself I wasn't worth saving. I now have to guess every one I love in my life and see if once the right time comes, they are going to betray me or back stab me just like she did. I am angry because people die of cancer without given the chance to live and make memories. I am angry because she is a waste of oxygen. She takes up living space that many others are in need of, and the saddest part about it. She doesn't appreciate it. None of it.

(Village Velikaya Znamenka, School #3)

Being an "orphan" did have perks to it. At our school, there were two orphans, me and this girl Yulia, whose mother just vanished on her, so she grew up with her grandmother. Our school cafeteria provided free lunches for Yulia and I, which did put a target on our backs and now kids were making fun of us for how we couldn't afford to buy lunch. Yet, years later, I began to sell my lunches to my rich classmates. Funny how the tables have turned. Every summer, Yulia and I would go to summer camps on the Black Sea. It wasn't just us two; there were orphan kids from the nearest towns and of course, kids whose parents could afford it. I was able to go to those summer camps on the sea until I turned eighteen, and before I was taken away by the system, I think I went for four summers in a row. The summer camp's location was never the same; they tried to switch it up for us every summer. The camp itself was three weeks long, and it was the best experience of my life!

One year, I went to summer camp, which was bigger than the one that I usually went to. Every summer camp, my grandmother tried to give me as much money as she could afford to bring with me. She would always tell me to be quiet about it because my grandfather wouldn't approve of it and most definitely take it away.

That summer changed my perspective on things and life in general. Every residential building had a divider in between. On one side of the divider were kids like me or kids whose parents paid for their kids to go to the camp. On the other side of the divider were orphanage kids. The director of the camp thought that it would be smarter to keep those kids all together instead of separating them. Once a day, the divider would get unlocked by the supervisors, allowing kids to go to the other side to meet new people. Otherwise, we would have to go around the building to access the same building just from another door. I didn't understand that at all. Keeping those kids all together just made them stand out more than they already did. I hated the system for doing that to them. I hated the fact that I was one of those kids who was afraid of those kids on the other side of the divider because they were just like me, who got marked with a label.

Every night, the camp would have a "discoteka", where the DJ would play some music and everyone would dance around, of course, it was supervised by our leaders. We got lucky with our leaders that year, whose names were Alina and Misha. I'm not sure about Misha, but Alina was about 22 years old and had a kind heart. Having discoteka at the camp allowed us to dress up, do our hair and feel like we existed on some other planet. Because this isn't something we get to do back at home. Every group had a certain number. The higher the group number, the lower the kids' age was. Depending on the age, that determined how long a particular group gets to dance and be present at the "discoteka." During the first week at that camp, my group was still dancing at the discoteka, but I was getting thirsty. I told my leader that I was going back to the room so I could get some water, and she offered to walk me for safety reasons, to which I laughed. I told her that I would be fine on my own. I shared the room with three other girls and my roommates, and I hated the location of our bedroom. The bedroom was between a toilet and the leader's room. So, we would always hear people taking poops and constantly hearing the toilets get flushed. Or we would hear our leaders have sex, to which we couldn't help ourselves but giggle. When I entered the bedroom, all of our mattresses were on the floor, and the whole room was a mess. It looked like we got robbed. The first thing I did was look into my backpack to see if the money that my grandmother gave me was still there; unfortunately, it wasn't. I went back into the hallway, and the first thing I did was look over at the divider; the door was unlocked. Without thinking, I marched to get to the other side. I felt confident; I felt like I was about to start World War III or win a fight. Yet, my heart was pounding. I was breathing heavily, and I was scared for life. Once my foot stepped on the other side of the divider, a leader came out of a room. He looked at me and said:

"Can I help you?", I could tell he was judging me in some type of way. I didn't know what to say, so I just kept walking towards the exit. As I was walking, a girl rushed out of a bedroom; she froze, and so did I. I could tell she was nervous by the way her body was responding; she couldn't stop biting her lip. I wondered if she could tell the same thing about me. I came closer to her and whispered into her ear:

"I know what your people did, and I'm not going to let it slide", and I speed-walked out of the building. As I rushed back to the dance floor, I heard a slow song, which could only mean one thing – everyone is slow dancing. Yet, the only thing that was on my mind was to find my roommates and tell them what happened. As I picked up my speed, that same girl who I ran into came out of nowhere and blocked my way and said:

"Who are you going to tell on me? I couldn't really hear you back there inside." Okay now I was scared for sure. The thing that came to mind was to scream; we weren't that far away from the dance floor so if I would scream "help" loud enough, someone would come to my rescue. But I didn't scream—not sure why. Instead, I walked slowly backwards. I continued to do so until I heard a girl's voice from behind me.

"Oh, look, she's scared." She laughed like a psychopath. I was about to run forward, thinking I could run pass them and we could continue this issue when I wouldn't be completely alone because two-on-one isn't fair at all. When I tried to start running, a girl behind me pushed me, causing me to fall onto the ground and scratch my hands, knees and face. I felt a tickle-like pain throughout my body.

As I was just lying on the ground, the girls laughed at me again and ran away. Leaving me looking like an abandoned puppy, "don't cry" I told myself. I stood up and ran to the dance floor; luckily, the first people I bumped in to were my roommates. I quickly explained to them what happened to me and what happened in our bedroom. They took me to our leader Alina because my lip was bleeding, and after freaking out, she took me to see a nurse. On the way, she was asking me all sorts of questions like who did that to me; when I told her the story, she called me stupid for not telling the leader what I saw happened. Which I kind of get. But every morning, while everyone sleeps, all of the leaders get together for a meeting where they discuss how things are going on and what needs to be done to improve.

Alina said she was going to bring this issue to the meeting. I'm not exactly sure what happened at that meeting, but what I know is that since that night, I haven't seen those two girls. I was told that it wasn't the first time they had caused trouble, so they were sent back to the orphanage. I felt bad for them. Because it was never about the money. It was about the fact that they did what they did because they didn't have anyone who could provide them with those types of resources.

One summer, just weeks before my summer camp, I was given a bike by my grandfather. It wasn't a brand-new bike, but it was nice to have something that belonged to me. I would go up and down the street as fast as I could, and my grandmother would stand outside our house in our front yard and watch me. There were nights when I came back with my knees scratched and covered in blood on my elbows because I was trying to learn how to ride with no hands like this girl next door did. I was so amazed by her. She would ride with both of her hands in the pockets of her jacket and wouldn't even fall or swerve. I wanted that to be me, yet till now, I can't ride the bicycle without at least one of my hands being on the wheel. I guess that's some kind of progress.

Before I left for the camp, I pretty much begged my grandparents to take care of the one thing that was officially mine: my bike. And they did. Well, they promised to. Yet, when I came back home from the summer camp, the bike was nowhere to be found. I couldn't stop asking my grandparents questions like where did it go? Did someone steal it? They didn't even care how heartbroken I was when they finally told me that they sold it because they needed to fight their hangover. They literally didn't care that they took one thing, which was MINE. Now, I was back to nothing. Not owning anything. And being nothing because I had nothing. Now, I was the one who sat in the front of the road in our front yard, watching other kids scratch their knees off learning how to do tricks.

Sometimes, what we wish for doesn't always end well… or the way we would expect it. On birthdays, what do you usually wish for? A new toy? Clothes? To go somewhere, you haven't been to. A cell phone? A puppy? Do you want to know what I wished for on my seventh birthday? I wished for a baby goat. I know what you are thinking right now. You might be laughing at me because who and why at age seven would wish for a baby goat?

I grew up in a small village. My grandparents weren't farmers no, but we did have a cow, chickens, and two dogs. I loved my dogs. One of them was named after my favorite cat, Rex, and the other dog, Donna, who was slightly aggressive. She was about two feet tall and gorgeous in many ways. Since she was a female, we would always get male dogs hanging out at our house. One time, my grandfather was going to work early in the morning, so when he was backing out, he didn't see Rex. Later that morning, I knew something was up when I asked where Rex had gone. Grandmother told me that he ran away. I knew she wasn't telling the truth because she couldn't look into my eyes as she was speaking.

I did have cats and dogs as pets at some point, but I always wanted a goat. The first time I wished for a goat was on my actual birthday in February. My grandparent's first excuse was, "Where are we going to get a baby goat in the winter, Kristina? It's not that easy, silly." I understood. That following summer, I asked if I could get a baby goat and not get any gifts for my actual birthday in the winter. To which my grandparents answered, "Kristina, we can't afford it right now." I understood. When the money problem was solved, once again, I wished for a baby goat. Their next excuse was, "Kristina, where are we going to put it?." At that point, I came to the conclusion that I would never own a baby goat. I never asked myself why I wanted the goat. Possibly because I never had one. Just the feeling of knowing that there is a chance of having and experiencing something new and unique.

My neighbors were two ladies in their 70s, and both owned several adult goats that were old enough to make milk. Luckily, I got to spend a lot of time with them. Since the neighbors' children lived in cities, to me, they seemed lonely, so I did my best to try to be around them. After school, if I didn't have much homework, they would invite me over to have a cup of tea and ask me how I was. Sometimes, I would help them with their goats because they had so much energy and wanted to run around, but the ladies were too old.

Yes, even though I spent a lot of time around goats, it was not the same as owning one. I wasn't able to do certain things with my neighbor's goats because they weren't babies and didn't play much anymore. At night, I usually would get home around 10 P.M. Obviously, I wasn't able to see their goats because they were sleeping in the shed. Spring that year changed me and just, in general, made me the happiest person ever. One of my neighbor's goats was pregnant and had three baby goats. Our neighbor Valya didn't need that many goats; she already had two female goats. I asked her if I could buy one from her, and she just gave me one. I remember myself running towards home with the best news ever to tell! I was hoping and praying that my grandparents would let the baby goat stay with us. As I ran home crazy, the dog started barking. Grandmother thought that there was a fire or something, but no, it was just me.

"Grandma, can I please, please, please, have it? You have no idea how happy I will be? Please, Grandma! You know, well, I always wanted one so badly," I almost started crying. I don't know if that was from happiness or just a thought that she would say no.

"Kristina, tell me what's going on? You scared me." She was in shock but was so calm at the same time.

"Okay, so our neighbor Valya said I could have a baby goat for free. Can you imagine? Can I please have it? I promise it will not die in a week. I will take care of it." She laughed, but I stood seriously and waited for her response. Finally, she nodded. You should've seen my face! That day after dinner, I was already playing with my baby goat. I decided to name it Rosa because the goat was a female. Every time I went to places like school or the lake, I would always hug my baby goat so tight that I was afraid something would happen to it. My grandfather enjoyed gardening, so at home, we had over forty different fruit trees from different countries: apples, plums, pears, many types of apricots, cherries, and so on. I even had my favorite tree, an apricot tree.

Believe it or not, but three months later, my baby goat was not a baby anymore. Rosa started to have little horns. So now when I tried to hug her, she would try to butt me with these. One time, I tried to ride her; at first, it was all right, but then it turned into something similar, as if I was riding a bull. Three months isn't a long time, but I loved Rosa with all my heart. It's unbelievable how in a short amount of time, I was so attached to the goat that I felt all that connection. I questioned why I would choose my pet instead of going to hang out with my friends.

THE BEGINNING OF THE CHILDHOOD ERA

I remember when I used to get into trouble with stealing some cabbage from the kitchen and for Rosa. When my grandma would ask where the cabbage went, I would say the dog ate it. She knew that I gave it to Rosa, but she would pretend that she believed me and jokingly would yell at the dog. That particular summer, I had a feeling. I had to leave for a summer camp for three weeks, and I didn't want to go. A feeling that if I go, something would happen to Rosa because since she was my goat. I was the one who would take care of it, give her food and water.

Three weeks at the summer camp went by quickly. I had an amazing time and even made many new friends. I don't think I have ever swam that much in my entire life. It was really hard to say good-bye, although there was something that kept me from crying and being all sad. Rosa. I was so excited to go home and see my goat! When my grandma picked me up, she did the "Grandmother thing." She started screaming, saying how much I changed in three weeks and how much she missed me. Finally, when grandma finished talking, I got a chance to ask about Rosa and how she was, but weirdly, she would change the topic to something completely off. I had no idea why. When we got home, I didn't even get a chance to see Rosa or put my bag down as my grandma asked me if I could run to the store and get some bread for dinner. On the way to the store, I saw my neighbor Valya. She kindly asked how Rosa was; I told her that I haven't seen her for three weeks and how excited I was to play with her when I got home.

When I got home it felt so empty.

I looked for Rosa everywhere, but I couldn't find her. I went to my grandfather and asked him if he knew where my goat was, to which he gave me a look. "Now isn't a good time." I kept looking for her and calling her name. No, respond. I went to my apricot tree to sit down and think.

As I came closer to my tree, I saw something that made my heart drop. On the lowest branch of the tree, I saw all that was left of Rosa. Two feet and a tail. I stood there as I was frozen and wasn't able to move. I wish someone could wake me up and tell me that all this was a bad dream, but no. When I touched the tail, all the memories came back, the first day when I just got her, and all these times of me trying to convince my grandparent to buy me a goat. I wasn't able to stand, so I started to run. I remember I was running fast as if someone was trying to catch me, and as I was running, I started to cry and scream. Rosa was the only thought that held my emotions, but since she was gone, I wasn't able to hold on to them, so I let it go.

I got home past dinner time, and my grandfather was sitting outside on the porch holding a bottle of beer, he looked at me like he was about to come to me and hug me tight, but no he did not. I kept walking by him. I went inside the house with one question still: why did they do this to me knowing how much that goat meant to me? I cried myself to sleep that night, and for a whole month, I was questioning every meal that I ate "Is that you Rosa?" Once again, sometimes what we wish for doesn't always end well or the way we expect it to.

CHAPTER 2
SILENTLY CRYING FOR HELP

As I adapted to the fact that my grandparents' home was my forever home. My mother liked to randomly show up at any time she pleased. Sometimes, it would be for a few hours; sometimes, it would be days. She would show up, ignoring the fact that she was causing pain every time she showed up in my life, and then leave all over again. But this time she was serious, believe it or not, I was the center of attention. She came all the way to say how she didn't want me in her life at all. Even though I wasn't a part of her life already, we went to court and made it all official. The judge asked my mom the same question over and over, hoping she would change her mind, "Naidenova Olga Vladimirovna, are you sure you want to give up all the rights of being a mother of Naidenova Kristina Vitalivna?" She kept saying "yes." Her face had no emotions, nothing. Afterward, she didn't even look at me and, my grandmother became my legal guardian. Since that day, I have been nothing, and more importantly, a nobody, to my mother. I lost value in myself. I told myself if my own mother didn't believe in me, then why should I? That was the day I started cutting myself. I would run away for an entire day, find dirty glass near a bus station, and I would cut myself over and over. Then I would cry, telling myself that I am nothing and will be nothing for the rest of my life.

Years later, I found out the real reason why my mother went to court and, in front of everyone, rejected me. Money. Since my "visiting" my grandparents turned into living with them permanently, I was an extra mouth to feed, and many years later, it didn't seem to go anywhere. This means that even though my mother would visit quite often, she didn't seem to want to bring me with her to start a new life. A life where we get to be a part of each other's lives on a daily basis. It didn't take a lot to convince my mother to tell the judge that she didn't want me.

Since the court case, my grandmother has been paid monthly for being my legal guardian. I am not fully sure where the money went, but every other month, we would struggle to put food on the table. Every now and then, my grandmother would ask our neighbors to lend us some food. Having my grandfather with alcohol problems for sure didn't help. Whenever he was in the "need" of getting drunk and there wasn't any money in the house, he would trade in things that had value. He would start small with my grandmother's jewelry, and then he couldn't stop. He wasn't able to fight it or control himself. He would go from small earnings to selling TV, vacuum, sugar, and anything that other people would want. Anything that would get him cash. Anything that would get him drunk. When my grandmother would get the money from the government that was supposed to "support" me, she would go back to those homes to buy our TV and other things back. It was truly humiliating.

In seventh grade, I got into the biggest fight with a girl who wasn't being quite polite to my friend's sister. We were taking the bus home, and it was her stop. She walked by my friend's sister and pushed her with her shoulder, ending up making a scene. I got off at her stop because I believed my friend's sister deserved an apology. I asked her politely to apologize, and of course, she said no. She was one of those girls who had everything she ever wanted or needed. She wasn't humble at all and loved gossiping about other people's business. She wouldn't apologize. Friendship meant more than a family. So, I threw the first punch. People got around us, taking their phones out, getting ready to press the "record" bottom. I never was into fighting. I asked her to apologize one more time; she shook her head as a no. I grabbed her long, black hair and smacked it against my knee. I broke her nose. She was spitting blood out. People were screaming my name like I had just won the championship or something.

"Bitch, I said apologize," I asked her again as my hand was still holding her hair. She mumbled "sorry" so quietly that only I was able to hear it. I let her go. Someone screamed, "That was awesome," or "You did good." I didn't pay attention to any of the comments; they weren't important to me. What was important was that I actually felt something. I had power, and people around me believed in me. Even though that was just one stupid fight, it was so important to me. I think the main reason why that was the moment where I "felt" something is because that was one of the rarest moments where those kids saw me for who I was— they saw me. A girl who was so much more than an orphan or the poor girl who lived with her grandparents, you know? I got home and went to bed like nothing happened that day. However, karma is a real thing.

The next morning, we got visitors. It was that girl and her parents. When her parents told my grandfather what I did, he wasn't even surprised; neither was I. Her parents asked me to go down on my knees and ask for forgiveness. I refused. She deserved it. My grandfather apologized instead. From that moment, I knew I was not getting out of payback. The second we got into the house, he slapped me. My face was on fire. I had trouble with balance. I fell.

He grabbed a wire from a vacuum and beat me up. I was screaming, crying, asking him to stop, but he wouldn't.

He beat me up till the point I was bleeding. Then, he used one of his famous lines: "You brought shame to our family."

My aunt is a literal carbon copy of my grandfather; the attitude and the way she would think and do things was just way too alike. Both of them are hardworking characters, and it's almost impossible to change their mind on something they already made a solid decision. My biological mom was more like my grandmother, which isn't a a bad thing, just the opposite of my aunt and my grandfather. Both of them found it very difficult to get up early in the morning.

If cooking daily wasn't grandmother's responsibility, she would spend the entire day in bed watching drama TV shows. Since my aunt was more like my grandfather, he loved her more, showed more affection, and overall had more respect. He couldn't stand my mother. Taking naps throughout the day was necessary for my grandmother, to which my grandfather's response was, "It's a waste of time." If my grandfather caught my grandmother napping twice in a row, he would ask her in an annoying and aggressive voice "What, are you sick?"

The answer always would be a no, to which my grandfather would raise his voice and demand that she should clean the house, do laundry, cook dinner, and do anything but sleep. He called my grandmother lazy. My grandmother, my mother, and I look identical. Meanwhile, my aunt grew up with my grandfather's ways; she was tougher than us and wasn't scared of dirty work. My aunt also wasn't afraid of my grandfather like we were. He never lifted even a finger on her. Yet, beating my grandmother was one of his own specialties. There was a time he was swinging at her and fake hitting her but stopping halfway, and she was so scared she pooped her pants, to which my grandfather responded with a laugh. Genuinely, my grandmother deserved an Oscar for living with such a monster, who made her life a living hell where she had to hide away from him just to have a moment to herself to take a breather.

I used to run away A LOT! Go to school and not come back home for days. Whenever I would ask my grandparents if I could spend time together with my friends and the answer would be "No," I would run away and not come back, once again. Not because I didn't want to, but because I was afraid. I was afraid of my grandfather. I had a perfect idea of what he was capable of. I knew if I came back home, he would beat me. The group of friends I was involved with was not the best.

Vera, Tanya, Tanya's sister Lena and later on Luba. They introduced me to their friends and showed me ways to stay alive, and run away from the police officers in times when needed. I fully understand why my grandparents wouldn't want me to spend time with the troubled kids. They wanted me to be something, and me spending time together with the troubled kids was not smart of me. Yet, I was a teenager. I was unstoppable. After hanging out for a couple of hours with my friends, I knew that their parents would let me spend the night if it was the weekend. Otherwise, I would spend my night outside, in the cold.

There were times when I would come home and spend the night outside with my dog named Dana in her doghouse, but sometimes, I wouldn't sleep at all. I would wander the streets looking through the windows, watching families watching movies and kissing their children goodnight. The next day, I would wear the same clothes as the night before, and people would know something wasn't right. Some parents wouldn't let their kids hang out with me because I was bad news. Funny how they had no idea how their kids made me be "bad news." At the same time, I do understand why some families didn't want to get involved with me.

One day I ran away, the usual. As the day was getting closer to turning into the night, my friends and I were playing hide and seek by the lake. This is where it's getting good. One of my friends got a phone call from her mom saying that my aunt showed up with a knife, screaming she'd kill the mother unless she told her where I was. Who would want to get involved with a child who has a crazy aunt like that? I know I wouldn't.

I tried. I really tried to be friends with my classmates, but they didn't want to be friends with me. I was a thief who stole from my own house. Even my grandmother tried. Before I got involved with those girls, I was friends with two boys for ages. Maxim and Gena. Maxim and Gena have been best friends since they were born, and Maxim was my classmate. My grandmother and his mom were somewhat friends, so me joining their boy gang was no big deal. Yet, after years, they began to make fun of us because we didn't own a car and because we were poor. There were days when I was a loner with no friends, but my grandmother understood me.

There was a girl who was also my classmate from a parallel group. Her name was Alena, and she was adopted. My grandmother thought that we would automatically click if we'd give it a chance because we have a lot in common. My grandmother thought it would be a good idea to force our friendship. She talked to Alena's parents one time, and they invited me for dinner at their place. But it didn't work out. Instead, I felt more loser than I had ever been. The way her parents treated her, cared for her, and loved her. Her parents were too rich for my standards, so they looked at people like me as a waste of time. After that dinner, I never went back, and at school, Alena and I pretend like that dinner never happened in the first place. Plus, she already had so many friends who were just like her, so she didn't need a loser in her group.

There was a time when I was going through my grandparents' jackets looking for spare change so I could get a beer with my friends that night. Yet, instead, I found something bigger… I found my grandfather's wallet. He had about 600 Grivnas with a note that said "Electric" and "Gas." I knew damn well what that meant and how badly we needed that money to keep our home alive and warm. I wasn't thinking straight. I didn't think for a second instead, I grabbed the money and ran. I ran so fast, thinking that any second my grandfather would go outside and see me run and go after me. I knew I would be dead if he caught me. I ran through people's gardens and their homes. When I got to Vera's house, I had a giant smile on my face and by the look on her face, she knew shit was going down. With that money, we bought so much booze and invited pretty much everyone to drink with us; we were telling everyone it was my birthday. For once in a lifetime, I thought, this is where I belonged. Guys were screaming, "Kristina you're the best!" and "Happy Birthday", and everyone was giving me hugs. At that moment, I felt alive. Towards the end of the night, the girls Tanya and Vera asked to hold on to the money in case I would lose it, and I remember them saying to my face, "Tomorrow morning, we are going to take a marshrutka to the city and go shopping." Tanya even offered me to spend the night at her place, which she never has before because of her strict mother.

Once the morning came around, the house felt empty, and that was half true. When I woke up, there was only Lena and me. When I began to question Lena about her sister and where she was, she didn't seem to be bothered at all. Soon enough, Vera and Tanya a taxi dropped them off and of course, I attacked them with so many questions, but importantly, where was the money. They just laughed in my face and said, "What money?" This is where I began to freak out and raise my voice because that was the moment it hit me damn well what my grandfather would do to me once he noticed the money was gone. I couldn't help but notice the new t-shirts and jewelry that they were wearing.

I sat down right next to Vera and asked her again, but this time calmly, where the money was. She took a deep breath, and I'm not going to lie, I was scared that she was going to hit me. But this time, she raised her voice at me and said, "Kristina, you need to calm down. It wasn't even that much money. Tanya and I just bought ourselves a few things and got lunch" as she was saying that, she was looking dead into my eyes. I could feel the tears pilling up in my eyes. I knew I fucked up big time. Then Vera added that maybe I shouldn't be so stupid to trust them to hold on to the money. I knew. I knew those girls only were doing what's best for themselves and no one else. I sat down and wished to bring the time back because the money that was put away for gas and electricity at my house was now used by strangers who only satisfied themselves. This was a time I wished to unknow them, but it wasn't that simple. Even though Vera and Tanya fucked me over more than once, without them I didn't think I would be anything. It's not that I had the whole world lying in front of my feet because I was friends with them, but at the end of the day I had someone. And that someone was still better than nothing.

Once, I really knew how deeply in trouble I was, and I was terrified to go home because I knew exactly what was waiting at home for me. A belt. After explaining the whole situation to Tanya and Vera, Vera felt sympathy for me, which was shocking for all of us. She offered me help. Her mother was really scared of my aunt, and she didn't want any trouble with the police. After her mother would go to bed, Vera would sneak me into her barn, and I would sleep with her goats on the straw. It wasn't the comfiest, but it could've been worse. In the morning, once her parents would go to work, Vera offered me a shower and food.

I lived in her barn for about a week until Vera's oldest sister caught me coming out of their barn covered in straw. She told Vera that if I won't go back home, she would tell their mom everything. Vera was not scared of their mom, in fact, they fought a lot. PHYSICALLY. Deep down, I appreciate everything that Vera did for me back then. I would watch her do her make-up and dress up every time we'd hang out with boys at night. She helped me look like a girl and not a boy by doing my makeup and painting my nails. She was there for me when I had nothing to offer in return. She was a friend.

After I could no longer spend the night in Veras shed, I had no idea where to go or who to go to. So, I would go back home, sleep in our outside shed that had no windows and no doors, just walls and a roof and sleep there. If I was lucky enough, I would find something edible. But this was a game changer for me, and it made me think I was actually smart and doing something. The shed had some of my clothes, which allowed me to change and look like a normal teenager.

One night, everything changed. I had a plan, just like any other night. To wait behind the house until the lights were turned off so I could make my move. However, that particular night, our storage dog, Dona, was too excited to see me. I slowly came near her and began to give her my love; within seconds, my heart dropped. The outside light turned back on, I ran and hid behind the house, hoping it was nothing. Minutes later, I heard my grandmother's voice; "Kristina? Is that you there? Please come out." Her voice was just straight pain to my ears. Without thinking, my body began to walk slowly towards her. We hugged. I burst into tears. I missed home.

Then, I snapped out of it. I took a giant step back and told her that I couldn't come home, and she knew exactly why. I remember she told me that she knew I was sleeping in the shed because some of the things were missing, and my dirty clothes were just piling up. I felt really bad for doing this to her, but I am a survivor. I had to do what's best for me, and it was to stay hidden from my grandfather, who was a very scary man. I came closer to the dog and hugged her goodbye. Within seconds, I felt my grandmother's arms around me, and I couldn't move. She looked into my eyes with tears in hers and whispered, "I'm sorry, but I gotta do what's best for me." I didn't even have time to blink as she screamed really loud: "VOVA, COME OUTSIDE! I GOT HER!!!" I kept screaming "Please let me go". But once I was in his arms, my grandmother walked away, saying how painful it's going to be for her to watch it. I couldn't move. He brought me into the house and locked the front door. Then he pushed me into another room and locked it behind him too.

On the stool there was a belt waiting for me already. He didn't even hesitate; he grabbed the belt and started beating me as hard as he could. Once I had the opportunity to escape from his arms, I hid under the bed. He stopped for a second, took a deep breath and went into another room. I didn't have the balls to come out because I knew it was far from being over. He came back into the room with a cable from our vacuum. He wrapped it around his waist, band over, grabbed my arms, and once the majority was out from under the bed, he began beating me with the cable. He didn't look where he was hitting my face, my arms, my stomach, my legs, whatever he saw. I couldn't stop crying and begging him to stop, but he wouldn't hear me. He began to scream back at me and throw "Slut!" "This is your grandmother's fault that you are just like your mother!" "Prostitute!" "Shame" with every hit, there was an assault followed by. Then, he stopped, grabbed my tiny face, screamed "Slut" one more time and spit into my face as he continued to beat me. He beat me until I bled. He didn't care and it seemed like he was never going to stop. I kept begging him to stop, but he wouldn't listen to me.

Luckily, my grandmother began to bang on the windows and scream "ENOUGH!" I could tell by her voice that she was crying too. He didn't listen to her either; instead, he told her to shut the fuck up. Every chance I got, I would bite him and go hide under the bed, but he would always get me and beat me even harder. My grandmother didn't stop banging on the windows, and once I was shaking and bleeding, hiding under the bed, my grandfather dropped the cable and screamed, "Get her out of my face; I can't even look at her." I didn't come out until I knew that he wasn't coming back. My grandmother walked me to the shed and cuddled me until I fell asleep. Of course, it was not until she gave me her side of the story that I realized how awful I had made it for her. Every night I was gone, my grandfather made her search the streets and not come home without me. She said she could feel that I wasn't anywhere nearby, but he wouldn't understand it, so she would walk the streets and cry while doing it. I cried even harder because she didn't deserve any of this. The person who was the love of her life ages ago was now a monster who was unstoppable and capable of scary things.

I couldn't go back to school for two weeks because my bruises were so bad. My grandmother had to lie to the school principal, saying that I had chicken pox. I couldn't sit down for days. Now I am twenty-four years old, and till today, I remember that night like it had happened last night; just thinking about it brings tears to my eyes. Years later, I still have one scar on my inner thigh from that night. It is a reminder of who I was and where I came from.

One time, my aunt brought some guy over named Sasha with her, telling everyone he is the one. He was covered in tattoos, but the tattoos that stood out to me were stars on each of his knees. The reason they stood out to me because my grandfather had the same ones in the same place. Sasha and my grandfather had a special bond, and later, I found out that weed was the answer to that. At some point, I considered my grandfather a role model, but when I found out that they were smoking weed - the thought of him being perfect was gone. Sasha and my grandfather would walk around the town shirtless, flexing their tattoos as if they owned the town. The story ends with Sasha stealing from us and running away; since then, we never talked about him. My grandfather would call my aunt stupid for falling for such an idiot, but when my aunt would mention the "good" times when theyhadmoking weed behind the shed, my grandfather would change the subject. Yeah, my grandfather was far away from being perfect.

At some point in my childhood, my aunt wanted to bring my mom home. She wanted to help her to find herself and tell her she could do better. Not surprisingly, my aunt ended up in the exact same place where my mom was. Sleeping with older men for money, drinking till the point of not knowing where they were, having the time of their lives. How does one go to a few cities and end up in Turkey? At that point, my grandfather had given up on me; whenever he would get drunk, he would yell in my face:

"You will be just like them. Get out of my face."

Whenever my grandfather would start drinking, my grandmother would try to make him stop, try to make him stop in any way possible. It never worked out. He would hit her, scream in her face, and call her names. After a while, she would give up and would become his drinking buddy. When my grandparents became alcoholics, there were nights when they would ask me to go out and buy them some homemade cheap alcohol.

In Ukraine, the drinking age is 18, but no one cares. Sometimes, my grandmother would write a note, then she would sign it, and I would go to the neighbors to get it. When there would be no money in the family, my grandfather again would try to sell stuff from our house. Anything that had value, such as TV, vacuum, my grandmother's jewelry, even sugar. He was addicted. Whenever my grandparents were drinking, it wasn't just a day or two. It was weeks and months without a pause. I didn't go to school; there was no point for me to do so unless I wanted to get more hate from my classmates. Sometimes, I would leave the house for days without my grandparents knowing; they never realized that I was gone for days; they were too busy drinking. Then, whenever he would get sober, he would yell at me or my grandmother because we didn't try to stop him; the truth is we did.

I reminded my grandfather too much of my mother and even my grandmother. We had the same face shape and shared too many similarities when it came to viewing behavior in life; since my mom was never around, my grandmother raised me pretty much all by herself. She taught me how to be and act around people, and as every day, every month, and even year went by, I began to act and look like my grandmother. Because of it, my grandfather stopped seeing his favorite granddaughter that I was. He began seeing his wife and daughter through me and hated me for it.

Before I started 1st grade, my grandfather would yell at anybody who would swear or yell in front of me. If the situation was getting out of control, someone would take care of me by putting me in another room and make sure I wouldn't hear anything. Yet, once my grandfather would get hammered so badly that he would forget my name, he obviously stopped giving fucks about what kind of language was being used in my presence or who was punching who while I sat at the dinner table doing my math homework. We, as a family, never bothered to go out to a local cafe or anywhere in public because my family was far from knowing how to be polite or show respect and kindness to others. New Year was the only holiday we would dress up for and try to celebrate like a normal family. But because my family is so full of alcoholics, I already knew that every celebration would look exactly the same.

Because of my family's alcoholism, we were well-known on every street in the town. My grandfather was known for beating my grandmother and me but also for taking everything out of the house and trying to sell it to literally anyone; then, the next morning my grandmother would get punished for not trying to stop him or to come up with a better solution on how to get alcohol. When my grandfather would get sober, and we'd finally have a little bit of money saved, my grandfather would force my grandmother to go back to those houses where he sold our home goods, like a fancy TV or a really nice vacuum that took about three pensions to pay off because we could never afford anything and try to re-buy them. You can imagine how stupid he made my grandmother look. At some point, this strategy got so old that the families that my grandfather sold our valuable products to ended up just putting everything aside because they knew damn well in a few months, we'd be back to re-buy it.

We never had money laying around or just being saved in a bank account. Never. We always owed money to someone, and when we didn't owe money, we owed our neighbors sugar, milk, bread, eggs, etc. There was always someone or something. The thing is, I didn't even know that my family was "broke", or "poor"; I didn't really understand the whole money situation. I knew that money was something that we either had or didn't. I understood that some families had more money than others, but I wouldn't consider ourselves poor. I thought that the things we did as a family were normal; for example, we never owned Q-tips. My grandmother would rip off a piece of cotton from her mattress and wrap it around a match, which worked just fine. We never used napkins or paper towels, never! We had one kitchen towel we would pass around if someone needed their hands wiped. When I would use my clothes instead of the towel, to which my grandmother would smack my head and scream, "Use the freaking towel." She hated when I would get my clothes dirty because that would mean she would have to wash more clothes. Hand wash, of course; we never owned a washer or a drier.

In summer, as a family, most of the time, it would be me and my grandmother; we would pick a day, most usually a Saturday, and we would hand wash all of our clothes. She was way faster than me at it, but at least now I know I don't have to panic when I run out of clean socks because I can just hand wash them.

One time, I was telling my guy friends about menstruation and how excited I was to get my period. I told them how my aunt uses pieces of cloth to prevent the bleeding. I remember their reaction so vividly, "cloths??" They both turned their heads at me with question marks on their faces. "Yeah?" I wasn't so sure what I was talking about now. I was confused because they made it seem like it was not normal. "Oh yeah, I forgot your family is poor, so you probably can't afford pads and tampons". They laughed in my face. "Pads and tampons?? What's that?" that language was so unfamiliar to me, it's like they weren't speaking Russian to me at all. "Forget about it; you can't afford it anyways."

I stood quiet with my head hanging down, looking at my feet. My pace slowed down, and I had nothing to say back to them. They were probably right.

In such a small village that I grew up in, where everyone knows everything about everyone, we help each other in times that are tough; when the other people are at the bottom, someone would always offer a hand. But you always have to return the favor. Because in such a small village rumors can be created really fast. It doesn't matter if those were false or true rumors, yet those rumors will make the whole town turn their backs on you quick.

I remember one time we were so broke we couldn't afford to put food on the table, and for a while, the local marketplace would loan us food in advance. At that point, the only money income we had in our family was my grandmother's pension and child support money that the government would send us monthly. With school supplies and clothes that I needed, there was barely anything left to use for groceries. When it came to school shopping, we couldn't afford anything shiny or fancy like the rest of my classmates. My grandmother and I would go to the Bazaar or a secondhand store and try to make it work, and it did work. I may not have had the cooler Adidas outfit or the brand-new shoes, but at the end of the day, I had clothes, and I was fed. My school, just like any other, treated it as if we didn't go there for education but for a fashion show. Meanwhile, everyone in my class knew my family. I could never participate or be a part of that "fashion show" because my clothes were never expensive enough as my grandparents couldn't afford to buy a new backpack every school year, so mine had holes. When winter came, my winter coat made me look like a homeless man because it was three times bigger than me, so it could last longer than just one winter.

Every grade had a class leader who was also a teacher at the school. A class leader is a person who the school would come to if the class was struggling with grades or if a particular classmate was in trouble. Then, after school or throughout the day, the class leader would get their grade together and lecture the class on how things are and what we'd need to do to get better. A class leader would be the one who would hand out diplomas at the graduation and the one who would hand out "good job" letters at the end of the school year if a student finished the year with excellent grades and good behavior.

Most of the time, the class leader would either get assigned to a grade or they would have the option to choose the first grade to lead all the way to graduation. From first to fifth grade, I have no idea who my class leader was, all I remember was that she's a woman, but that's about it. Yet, in sixth grade, we got a new history teacher who happened to be our new class leader; his name was Sergey Kraushkin. It didn't take him long to know my family and what my family is like. Once I got to the eighth grade and our class leader would teach history to us, he would give me free slides and just give me straight 12's on homework assignments without even actually reading it. He used to pull me aside and tell me that I did an excellent job because I at least did it.

In Ukraine, the grading system works on a scale of 1-12, where 12 is excellent, and 6 is barely passing. Students would get 2's for bad behaviors sometimes and when I would come home with a 2 in my journal, I would get beaten with the belt. By the time I was an eighth grader, all of the teachers had given up on me and my education altogether, yet Sergey Kraushkin was the only one who fought for me and my education till the last day before I gave up on myself and was taken away by the system. Sergey Kraushkin had hope for me, and I 100% trusted him. I went to him when I had home problems, and he simply understood me.

The school system in Ukraine is funny and very different from the States. School starts on the exact same day every year, September first. On September 1st, girls and boys must wear black and white. White tops and black bottoms, and to make the outfit more beautiful, all girls must wear bows in our hair. Each grade would get lined up with their class leader in the front; the parents would hide in the back for moral support. After a big ceremony, the class leader would get all the parents together in the same room and discuss what we would need as a class. This means new curtains, new chairs, money for National and Women's days and also birthday gifts.

A week or so after that big meeting, every student must donate about 200 grivnas for those things. I would always donate later than everyone else because we never had an extra 200 grivnas to donate. In times when I was really late, my class leader, Sergey Kraushkin, would donate the money to me. Once in a few months, we would have a follow-up meeting where a family member had to come for every student. In those class meetings, the class leader would talk about every student's behavior and how they are doing in school. My grandfather never went to a single class meeting. It was always my grandmother, and when she wouldn't show up, and I had to sit by myself at my desk, everyone knew something was wrong again. It was one of the most disgusting feelings ever, knowing that to the left and right, everyone was whispering and talking shit about me and how terrible my family was. Little did they know that it was all not my fault that I was born into a family full of alcoholics and not rich people who have caviar every morning and drive fancy cars instead of taking public transportation because it's "too gross" and "unsanitized."

My school had one janitor, and their job was only to clean public places like halls. Our school had one bathroom for students, and it was outside. No stalls, no toilets, just six holes in the ground. We, as a class, were responsible for cleaning inside our classrooms. The class leader would make a schedule of who would have to stay after school to clean the classroom; most of the time, it would be a boy and a girl. One time, I stayed after school to clean with this new boy in our grade. I remember specifically that I was mopping the floor and within seconds, that new boy was standing covered in that dirty floor water for his big dirty mouth. I was pretty much out the door with the bucket in my hand when he opened his mouth and said to my face, "So I heard your mom is a slut huh?"

I stopped for a second and turned around, and now I was facing him. "What did you just say" I heard what he said the first time, but the audacity?! Without hesitation, he came closer to me and repeated his exact words to my face. The bucket full of dirty water was now on his head, and his new gray sweater was soaking. I grabbed my stuff and walked away. The next day, you can imagine that the boy's parents called the school and wanted to meet up with my grandmother. To which our class leader had to call an emergency parent meeting; those are the worst because it is one-on-one, and the meeting itself is full of accusations towards my family and me. Apparently, when I put the metal bucket on his head, the metal cut his ear, and he came home with a bleeding ear. My grandmother and I left the meeting with the title of being monsters.

Our school had one school bus. We had main stops where students would meet up to wait for the bus, and the driver would just scoop us. Yet, the wintertime was always a guessing game. Winters in Ukraine can get terrible. When the school bus would break, we had no way of knowing. From my house, the ride to school was about twenty minutes, but those who live on the last drop out stop live about forty minutes driving. When the school bus wouldn't show up on time, some of the students would go home and their parents would drive them. Yet, the rest of us, like me, who had zero sources of transportation, would have to walk to school. Walking to school would be about an hour of slow pace. By the time we got to school, we would have made it to the second period.

The end of the school year was my favorite time of the year because, most of the time, I choose to walk home. Walking on the sidewalks where the trees were full of fruits, like cherries, plums, and apricots. So peaceful. Until some owners would run out of their properties and scream your way, "STOP STEALING!" Sometimes, I would get distracted by the abandoned mansions by going inside them and just pretending those houses are being built for my family and me. My grandmother hated it when I walked home from school. She would go outside and wait for me to get off our stop, but she wouldn't find me in the crowd. With no sources of communication, she had no idea where I was, who I was with or what time I was getting home. Most of the time, I would get home within thirty minutes to an hour after the school bus dropped off everyone else.

Our family friend Olga lived in one house down the road from us. She was a single mother and was the same age as my aunt and Mom, so they always spent time together. Most of the time, partying. At that time, she only had one child, a son named Jenya. Since our mothers and families in general spend most of their time together, we did too. Occasionally, I would sneak to their place late at night until my grandmother noticed that I was missing, and she would find me quickly and know that there was one place I could be at. But as Jenya and I grew up, we became runaway buddies.

One time, when my grandfather was getting sober, I ran away with Jenya. We ended up wandering around the center of the town asking elder people for coins so we could buy a snack. Once we were on our way home, his mom found us and brought us home by bicycle. I knew exactly what I got myself into, so I was ready. When I got home, my grandfather was already waiting for me. He had this serious look on his face that the face itself would give me chills already. It was a long pause before he said anything; he was just staring at me. Finally, a question: "Why did you run away?" I was afraid to answer him, so I didn't. He asked me that question again, but this time, he slapped the table so hard I jumped. I didn't answer him; I ran instead. Surprisingly, he went after me. When he caught me, he picked me up and threw me against the ground like I was a homeless cat or a piece of garbage - not a living soul. He picked me up and threw me repeatedly, then he looked at me, spit and left me lying on the ground. I wasn't crying or screaming anymore; at that point, I was in shock, trying to process what happened. I had difficulties moving my right hand. We called the town doctor, and when they asked what happened, I was quiet. I didn't know what was okay or not okay to say. When actually none of this is okay! My grandfather said I fell. When the doctor left, my grandfather went on his knees and apologized, but he wasn't looking into my eyes or at least towards my direction, so I knew he didn't mean any of the words he told me.

My grandparents have threatened me before. Threatened me with words, with lazinas (a thin branch that I got my ass beaten with), as well as physically. They had threatened me with orphanage shows and news that we should see on the

TV, even with the police. I never believed them, or maybe I did believe them. I just didn't think that they would have the actual guts to either actually kill me or to send me away willingly. Before I turned into a monster, I was their precious little girl. Their only grandchild. But, outside of everything I listed above, they still found a way to make my life even more miserable. They thought that cutting all my hair and making me completely bald would make me ashamed enough of myself, enough that I would stop running away. Like I said, I was a monster, I was unstoppable, and I admit it, I really do. But as grown people, they should've known what it would do to a child. WHO'S A GIRL! What it did to me!!!

One time, my mom randomly showed up at our house with a bunch of goodies and a man. She introduced him as her new husband, even though he was around 40 and she was very young. She seemed to really like him, or that was just for the money, I couldn't really tell. They spent the night at our place; then, he invited me over to check out where he lives and meet his family. I told him I would, but only if my mom would come with us; he said she would show up later. She never did. I met his family. Everything was nice and for once, I thought that this man could be my father, even though he already had a family. After dinner, he would have a drink or two, then… he touched me in places he shouldn't touch a ten-year-old girl. In the morning, he would apologize and even try to take my mind off by buying me a new phone, but then the cycle would repeat at night. After two days, I got a call from my mom. She was wondering where I was, so I told her I was with her friend and that we were waiting for her. Her reaction? She yelled at me for trying to steal her man. I never told her what he did to me; I knew she would laugh and tell me I was making it up, that he would never. So, I didn't; the next morning, I got home, and trouble was already waiting for me. When my aunt saw my new phone, she threatened to take it away from me so she could use it herself since I was "too young." The man just disappeared out of our lives. My mom just moved on to the next rich man.

So far, you have been reading, you may think "Oh that's messed up; this girl has been through so much", yet there's so much more to it that it is just impossible to put fourteen years of life on paper. I didn't ask for anything on Christmas, birthdays, or New Year's because my family couldn't afford it. We would celebrate it, everyone would get slammed before 12 P.M and would fall asleep or pick a fight with each other, and I would be the one who gets to clean up all the mess. The scariest thing that I had experienced throughout my childhood was seeing my grandmother drunk. Whenever she would have a couple of shots, she'd cry and talk to her son, who had drowned a week before his 18th birthday. She'd sit, look far, and talk to him for hours; she told me that she could see him. I would cry because I was so scared I didn't know how to react, so I would run away and be alone with my thoughts. Walking down the street during the night, seeing happy families celebrating through the windows, and just being there with each other. My family wasn't able to manage that. We were never close to clarifying as a "Happy family."

A year later, around my birthday, Mom showed up with another man, but this time, he was somewhat closer to her age. She told me she was in love, but from what I saw, they were just drinking buddies. Even though she wasn't allowed to see me at all, she was risking her life - since she wasn't my legal guardian, the government took all her privileges from her, and that included even seeing me. She told me all the crazy stories where she lives now, by the beach. How she sees a sunrise every morning and how beautiful it is in winter. I wanted to see it!

CHAPTER 3
LEAVING EVERYTHING BEHIND FOREVER

I was a very troubled kid. Half the shit I did in Ukraine I for sure wouldn't be able to get away with here in the States. I very much regret what I did to my family and what I have put my family through. Both ends of this story have hurt each other; we may never know or truly understand which story started first and who's the one who should be at fault. BUT that absolutely gave them no right to cut all my hair out. My family had no idea what it did to a girl looking like a boy in a school full of boys. It was summer, most likely after noon. We were outside.

My grandmother, my aunt and my grandfather — the three musketeers, you shall say, all three of them had a role in this very lovely afternoon adventure. My grandfather was sitting on the bench smoking a cigarette, drilling a hole into my skull with an "I told you so" face. At first, my aunt held me down to a chair as my grandmother cut all my hair. I was not able to fight or even look into their eyes. I was screaming. Screaming as if I was getting cut open alive. At that moment, they were all monsters who had just kept ruining my life. I did not have much to offer, but they kept taking and taking little by little everything, I had. My eyes were down, and I could no longer resist. My tinny body was just on top of the chair that almost felt numb. Nonexistent. My tears kept falling down into the piles of my thin brown hair that was now on the floor. They were stepping all over it, and they didn't care. As my tears were falling down, the words that sounded like a heavy storm beating on a roof were now beating against my brain

"It is for your own good," "Kristina, do you hear me?" My aunt was trying to make it sound as if I volunteered to be in this position. Okay okay okay I hear you; maybe my action has provoked this a bit, but did they though? Was I so terrible that they had to take one thing away from me that made me feel like a girl? They absolutely had no other choice??? They HAD to make me bald, so I would hate myself just like everyone else did everywhere I went as if I didn't already. Wasn't getting bullied enough at school for being fatherless, having an alcoholic family, being an orphan? I mean, the list could go on, and the funny thing is… I didn't sit them down in the chair, or hold their arms down so they couldn't fight, and most importantly, I didn't take their self-respect and dignity. I didn't ask for those things. Yet I got punished for simply - existing.

The second the sound of the buzz cutter stopped, I ran… No. I didn't run away, and I wish I had. But my legs wouldn't let me. I was embarrassed. I ran into the house. Slowly, I dragged myself to what felt like forever until my eyes met hers… tears were rushing down my burnt cheeks. I felt frozen. Yet so seen at the same time. Seen by myself. My eyes were locked. Slowly. Very slowly, I lifted my arms up and touched my now bald head. My heart was running a marathon. And just like that, my mind snapped and sprinted in one direction. And the one word that kept coming out of my mouth was…

"UGLY" "UGLY" "UGLY" "UGLY" "UGLY" "UGLY" "UGLY" "UGLY" "UGLY" "UGLY" "UGLY"

I could not shut myself up. Truly? I don't think I wanted to because I didn't know who I was staring at, but one thing I did know was that I hated that girl. She was the ugly duckling from that tale except this one didn't have a happy ending.

Weeks later, after my bald head wasn't so bald anymore some small hair were peeking through. I was starting to look more like a human. After a few drinks... who am I kidding?! Even sober, my grandfather would call me over and say, "Come here boy", or "Where is my boy at?" and when I came over, he would grab my head and do the scratching thingy with his knuckles you have seen dads do to their sons. Maybe deep down, he felt that he got his son back? It might've been all cute and everything for HIM, but for me, it was just another punch in the face.

Maybe I was ugly, but I wasn't stupid... it wasn't long before I planned my geniuses'run-away plan. My plan took a whole of about five minutes to plan by the way. What can I say?! I am a natural. We were in the middle of cleaning out the attic and in a million years, you would not guess what I found. My mother's wig. You might've seen a dirty old wig, but I saw an opportunity. You know what it felt like? You know those American idol shows, or Britain Got Talent? I know we have one in Ukraine called "Ukraine's Got Talent." Well, anyway, in those shows, if you move on to the next level or whatever, they give the ticket, right?! Well, that's what it felt like, like I got that damn ticket.

I put on that nasty wig, and I sprinted. I ran for my life. This plan was 10/10 and nothing less. It was perfect until it wasn't. Because I ran to only where I thought I would be acceptable for who I was. I ran to Vera and Tanya. Of course, after a few what felt like years of them laughing and making jokes and even touching my boy-looking head, they accepted me. Or so I want to believe that. But the wig was so huge on my head after a while it no longer worked; it kept falling off or people kept yanking it off. I got so damn tired I just threw the wig away and accepted it. People were still staring and pointing fingers, but at least now – if it wasn't "our" people, the rest of the people were getting threatened to get hurt. Vera kept saying, "only we can make fun of you." I mean ideally, I wouldn't want to get made fun of by anyone. But the sad part was that her words made me feel safer and more comfortable than I was at my own house.

Spending the whole summer with people who got used to me being bald was somewhat normal, but the thought of me going to school while looking like absolutely a boy was making my lungs come up to the top of my throat, making me choke again and again.

Once September rolled around, I wished it was any other month but this one. Going to school felt like walking on needles. Between classes, we had five and ten minute breaks. Yet, to me, those breaks felt like an eternity. Every single break, if I didn't get a chance to run out of the classroom, the boys would be on it right away, pulling my platok in every direction they pleased. It hides my bald head. I borrowed my grandmother's headscarf, which of course, drew more attention to me because now my school had a boy-looking girl who also looked like a babushka?! This practically screamed, "BULLY ME".

When spring came, I was ready. I had ten grivnas (Ukrainian money) in my pocket and was ready to hit the road. I told my grandmother I was going to school when, in reality, I was on my way to find my mom and live the life she lived. I didn't know where to go or how to get there. I didn't have enough money for the bus ticket, so I walked west for hours, hoping I was walking in the right direction.

I walked and walked for hours. Once in a few hours, a car or two would drive by me. As I walked, I passed a few older people who were peacefully working in their gardens. I asked for help with directions, where to turn or where to keep walking straight. Some people would look at me with an unexplainable look on their faces and say, "You are walking there?" or "Don't go there, there are wolves!" I wasn't fully sure if the people were telling me the truth or if they were trying to scare me away because I was just a girl who looked like she was on the run. When I'd tell them that I was on my way to find my mother, some old ladies were nice enough to give me a piece of bread or a glass of water. Yes, I was scared to death and had a bad feeling about it, but I also knew there was no way back. I kept telling myself that I wasn't weak and that it was time to prove that to myself. I was worried that I would get kidnapped or possibly killed. God was with me.

After hours of walking, I reached the bus stop. There was a guy age 18-ish, talking aggressively on the phone, not losing a chance; I approached him and asked if he knew what time the next bus was coming; his response was somewhat interesting.

"Don't worry, we are going to leave soon", he said. Yet, who's going where, and more importantly, with whom, I had no idea. It was getting darker outside, which made me more nervous. After ten-ish minutes, a fancy jeep pulled up, and the guy began to walk towards it, then he stopped and looked in my direction.

"Aren't you coming? Let's go." I started to walk slowly. Here it is, I thought. Tonight is the night I would get kidnapped, yet I kept walking towards the jeep. Once I got into the car, my eyes met with two big, bald guys.

"Who is she?" they asked.

"I don't know, but she looked lost; we will give her a ride."

I didn't say a word until one of the guys asked me

"Where are we dropping you off?"

"The center of Ushkalka." as I answered, I turned away to the window, praying I would see my mom soon.

I'm not sure how, but…No one kidnapped me. No one hurt me. I made it safely to my mom's town. When I got to the town, my expectations were way too high. The village was really poor looking and had only two stores: a cobbler and a mini food market. I was a little in shock; it was really different from the town where I lived. I expected to see lots of big stores, maybe a little park where parents would watch their children playing at the playground, a nice pond where old couples would feed the birds. No. Nothing.

"So how am I exactly going to do this?" I asked myself aloud. How am I going to find my mom without knowing her address, her boyfriend's name, or even if she was in town at all? I went to the first house I saw and knocked on the door. The guard dogs were barking crazy. A young lady opened the door.

"How can I help you?" the young lady looked at me like she had never seen snow before. I couldn't talk. I forgot how to speak at that moment, so I stood there like a tree, waiting for her to say something again. She didn't. She was standing and looking deep into my eyes like she was trying to read through me. I took a deep breath and asked:

"Hi, I am looking for my mom. Her name is Naidenova Olga, she's blond?!"- I said that with hope. Hoping that the young lady would answer me back with

"Oh yeah, I do know her, so let me show you where she lives." But that's not the answer the young lady gave me…

"No, I don't know her," as she slapped the door in the front of my face. All right, I thought, moving on to the next house. I knock, dogs are barking, and the circle repeats. This time a man opened the door and looked at me like he knew me, so he was looking at me like he was trying to remember me.

"Did you get lost?" he asked.

"Hi, I am looking for my mom. Do you possibly know Naidenovy Olga?" I asked once again with hope.

"Is she blonde?"

"She is!!!" I had a little excitement in me.

"Hold on, I'm going to tell my wife to take you over to where she lives." He closed the door, so I waited. Thoughts attacked me as I stood there and waited for about 10-15 minutes. What if I looked too suspicious, and he's going to call the police officers? What if he's going to kill me? What if he's going to kidnap me and then kill me? What if he's going to sell me? The door brought me back to earth. The door opened to a lady in her 30's.

"What is your name?" She asked, trying to start a conversation with me.

"Kristina," I answered probably being a bit short, letting her know that I didn't want to answer her other questions. I just wanted to see my mom. She gave me a ride on a bicycle, and thankfully, the ride wasn't long. When we finally got to the house, I stood there staring at it.

"Well, Aren't you going to go? It's your house."

"Right," I didn't sound so sure. I had no idea what I was putting myself into. What if my mom didn't want to see me? What if she wasn't home? What if she called my grandmother to pick me up? I was scared. My hands were shaking. I knocked on the window and waited. I was waiting for someone to come out and let me in. I didn't have to wait long at all. A woman in her 60's opened the front door.

"Hi, I'm looking for my mom. My name is…" she didn't let me finish my sentence.

"I know who you are. You look just like her," the woman jumped at me with hugs and kisses, and even though that wasn't the welcoming I had imagined in my head, I felt safe. Safer than when I was on the road...

"Come on in. Are you hungry?"

"Just a little bit"- I didn't eat all day, of course, I was hungry!

"She's right there" The lady showed me a room where my mother was. So, I slowly walked in like I was afraid something bad would happen. My mother was sleeping. I sat next to her and hugged her tightly from behind, which woke her up and now she was facing my direction. The second she realized it was me, she jumped:

"Are you real?"

"Yeah, I'm real" I laughed and hugged her again. She didn't hug me back. Maybe she was still in shock about the fact that it was really me hugging her, or she just didn't want to. I do not know...

"Does Grandma know you're here?"

"No! She doesn't! Please don't tell her! Please!" the second I was begging her not to tell Grandma where I was, she got a call. It was my grandmother... She was crying on the other end, saying how much I hurt her every time I ran away. I felt bad, but I NEEDED to see my mother and be away for just a few days.

I spent two weeks at my mother's house. We went to the beach, watched sunsets, cooked, and did everything together. For the first time ever, it felt like I had a connection with my mom; for the first time, it seemed like she had never gotten rid of me, and I'm sure if you'd look at us from the side, you'd think we are best friends. We weren't. Since my mom wasn't a legal parent to me, she had to pay some money towards child support, my education, and life in general.

LEAVING EVERYTHING BEHIND FOREVER

One day, my perfect life had come to an end. The police showed up at my mom's house with my grandmother. Since my mom hadn't paid the bill for a while, the government found out and wasn't happy about it. So now, try to imagine this picture. The dogs were barking like crazy, so here I am without suspecting anything. I open the door, and my eyes find my grandmother and two police officers. My heart dropped. My grandmother lost it. She had a heart attack. It wasn't a pretty picture.

The police took me and my mom to a police station in my town, which was in Kamenka Dneprovskaya. The system was really happy to "shut me down," as they said it right to my face. No more calls from my family telling them that I had been missing for more than three days, no more calls from the school reporting that I hadn't attended school in a week, no more neighbors complaining that my grandparents were drunk and me walking around the town with bruises all over my body. An hour later, mom came into the office, giving me hugs and kisses. Who knew she was saying goodbye?!

The police officers told my grandmother they would take me to a shelter, and the ride would take about four hours, so they sent her out to get me some snacks. The second she left, the police officers pushed me into the vehicle, and we left. I didn't get a chance to say goodbye to someone I loved the most. I didn't think about it until months later…

I was sitting in the back seat, looking back at the city. Who knew that was the day I was leaving my hometown and everything behind forever.

CHAPTER 4

BLENDING IN

The name of the town where my shelter was located was Melitopol. When I saw the sign "Welcome to Melitopol," I realized that I had never been THIS far away from my home. When we got to the shelter, security people searched me, making sure I wasn't bringing any illegal stuff on campus; besides that, people seemed nice. Not even ten minutes at the shelter, I heard a scream,

"Kristina? Is that really you?" As I turned, I saw my friend Luba; we used to run away together all the time. We hugged and smiled at each other for a long time. I hadn't seen her since the system took her away.

"Here we are," I said. Our families and teachers warned us about this type of life. They told us if we didn't stop running away, the system would take us, but we never believed them. There was the moment the system took both of us, and it was our fault.

I was alone in an empty room for a week. It is called "isolation" zone. The doctors were doing a check-up, making sure I wasn't sick and or didn't have any allergies or something that could possibly affect others. After a week, the doctors sent me to live in "Chistaya Grupa" (Clean Group) with the rest of the kids; there were 60 ish of us of all sorts of ages. I was excited to actually meet people and see my friend Luba again. In "Clean Group," I saw a lot of wild things, such as older boys beating each other and girls pulling each other's hair. Sometimes, I wouldn't get why those girls would fight each other over a boy or something as small as a t-shirt. But for some kids, a t-shirt could be something that's all they had ever owned, also memories…I saw a lot of stealing of course. Girls and boys would steal from one another, and the messed up part is the fact that the next day, they would lie about it or pretend like nothing happened and just continue the friendship. I guess that's when I slowly began to realize that this was my new reality too.

I remember one morning, all the girls had to line up for the monthly lice check-up. I remember exactly how fast my heartbeat was when the teacher opened the girl's (in front of me) hair, and we saw the biggest lice… I mean, I wanted to scream… At night, the boys would smoke cigarettes in the bathroom, and the whole floor would smell horrible.

After a few months of being at the shelter, I got used to all those things. I got more comfortable with other teenagers. One day, I asked a guy if I could make a call… Slowly, I dialed a ten-digit number and took a deep breath before pressing the green button to start the call, but hearing my aunt's voice on the other end was the definition of heaven. She said that she would try to do everything to get me back. She gave me hope. No people judged me at the shelter because we all were there for a reason, mostly for the same reasons. Stealing, skipping schools, parents didn't care, or parent's drug and or alcohol addictions.

I was at the shelter for 8 months. Everyone knew me, and honestly, I want to say that the staff loved me. Obviously, every staff member had their favorite, but every now and then, a few of the janitor ladies would bring homemade food just for me. And late at night, while everyone was asleep, they would invite me to their janitor's closet for a cup of tea with some delicious cookies.

Weirdly, I enjoyed spending time with older people more than kids my age. Usually, a teenager doesn't stay longer than a year at the shelter, but since I was there for

8 months already, every day could have been my last day. And that day came sooner than I expected it. I got called down to see the principal of the shelter, and they asked me questions about the orphanage. I remember losing hope. I remember crying at nights, telling myself that my aunt was lying about getting me out. Seeing teenagers getting picked up was hurtful. I remember telling the principal that I wanted to go to the orphanage located as far from my hometown as possible. I was mad. I was hurt. I was lost. And most importantly, I was alone.

My orphanage was located in the city of Zaporizhzhia, only 1.5 hours away from the shelter. There were 300 of us, from 4 years old to 18 years old. The first days at the orphanage were tough. I struggled a lot. It's like switching schools or moving to a different state. The building, which was full of bedrooms, had three floors. On the first floor, there was a washing room where the clothes would mysteriously go missing after the wash lady would give them a wash. A medical office is where we had our check-up appointments. This is the place that we'd go to get our morning vitamins before breakfast and any prescriptions if we had any. The first floor also had two isolation rooms, one of which was being used if someone was sick or, for example, had lice and can't be surrounded by other people to prevent the spread. This isolation room was nice; sometimes, teenagers tried to be put in it on purpose to ignore the class work or classes in general. It had a mini kitchen, three beds, a shower and a HOT TUB! The second isolation room was used for punishment. Why, you may ask? Because the size of the room is big enough for four beds, a sink, and a toilet - all in one room. The rest of the rooms on the first floor were used for kids who were in daycare. The second floor was strictly for girls. Third floor, yes, as you may guess, was all boys. The second and third floors each night had supervisors who watched the floor and made sure that there weren't any situations that needed to be taken care of. Teachers would go home after classes, and class supervisors would go home after dinner. Night supervisors were responsible for ensuring everyone was in their bedrooms and was alive by the morning.

My first night ever at the orphanage went wrong, and not how I pictured it. After the night supervisor announced that it was bedtime, I went to the bathroom to hand wash my sweater, which was covered in dirty stains. I was minding my own business as I was scrubbing the soup stains; the night supervisor walked into the bathroom and screamed at me "WHAT DO YOU THINK YOU'RE DOING?!!". I was so scared I dropped the sweater out of my hands onto the floor. She picked it up and started beating me with my wet, soapy sweater. I ran back to the room, yet she followed behind me. After I got in my bed, I was confused about what just happened, because since when washing your clothes is a crime?? She put my soapy sweater on the chair next to me, whispering, "You can finish it tomorrow once the sun is up." My heartbeat wouldn't stop racing for minutes. I stared into the dark, and after a while, I fell asleep to the water dripping onto the ground from my wet sweater. In my grade, there were 13 of us. 11 boys and 2 girls, including me. I never had a relationship with my classmates, at least not in the beginning. All the guys did those stupid pranks, like stealing my school bag or hiding my pens under the desk. I know what you are thinking right now, they did that because they were flirting because I was that "New girl." No. That wasn't it.

BLENDING IN

In the photo: Bottom of the slide (my classmate & friend) Anya and myself (top). This photo was taken at the orphanage playground. Anya was shortly adopted to an American family; and now living in Michigan.

At the orphanage, it doesn't work that way. Whenever there is a new guy or a girl in the class, the rest of the classmates try to figure out who they are as individuals, where they belong, and with what group they should hang out with. When I was that "new girl," I wasn't able to stand up for myself at the time. Why, you may ask? I was afraid. What can a new girl do or say to eleven guys? Now, you're probably thinking I could've told a teacher or someone who had more power than me and eleven guys. Yes, you are correct, but then I would have gotten made fun of for not being able to stand up for myself. I knew that months later, they would stop - and they did.

JOURNEY OF A RUNNING GIRL

In this photo: the orphanage; the bottom floor was occupied by the kindergarten class. The rest of the building was mostly used as bedrooms. The second floor was also occupied by girls and the third floor – boys.

I could write a book about my orphanage life, but that isn't my point. What comes to your mind when you hear the word "Orphanage?" I'm sure it's not the prettiest picture if you watched some documentaries on TV or some TV shows where they sugar coat or don't even do the justice of what it truly feels like living at the orphanage. But I guess it's either a huge family with 300 kids as one, or it's a jail with bars on windows. There isn't any between. It all depends on what perspective you are looking at it. I've spent almost three years at the orphanage, and I can tell you all about it… It's been ten years since I left the orphanage; however, till nowadays, I remember the smallest details. Every Friday for dinner, we'd have fish with mashed potatoes. We'd have the Ukrainian soup borscht on Monday, Wednesday, and Friday for lunch- no changes, no nothing. There were times when the food would get so boring that eating the exact same thing all over again wasn't great. Some days, my roommates and I would skip breakfast just so we could sleep for an extra 30 minutes.

Monday through Friday, we would obviously go to school from 9 am to 3 P.M. Then, free time, homework, dinner, shower if there is no line, bed. The next day - repeat.

From what you have read so far, that doesn't sound as bad, right? The orphanage could also mean you can't leave your phone in the hall to charge unattended. A simple five minutes - boom it's gone, and you will never see your phone or the charger ever again. Even a hair straighter, shampoo sucks — anything that could be useful to someone who doesn't have enough. It doesn't mean you have to watch everything, because it could happen at any time of the day or even at night. It could be your roommate taking the last shampoo you have, or it can be your caretaker stealing your socks so she could bring it home for her son/daughter.

(In the photo, the kids are from Matveevkie orphanage. Concert celebration towards New Year).

Orphanage. One word - yet, so many ups and downs. The orphanage taught me how to stand up for myself or to help others when they needed it. It taught me how to live in a community. "Sharing is caring" became one of the sayings I have lived by ever since. The orphanage taught me that life isn't full of sunshine and that there's always a dark side to everything. The orphanage taught me that I wasn't alone. That there are millions of children who lived the life I did, who needed a family and who still do. Orphanage taught me that life doesn't always have a happy ending. Orphanage was a reality check for me.

It didn't matter if we came to the orphanage with the same backgrounds or stories because at the end of the day, the orphanage meant something different to us.

Dima Gaponov, who was adopted from the same orphanage as me into a loving Ukrainian family here in the States, and here is what orphanage meant to him:

"*The word orphanage itself has changed for me over the years. It meant something different while I was at the orphanage, and it means something different now. Back then, the orphanage meant- darkness. I lost my family, and I lost everything that I loved. It was a place with no love. I had nothing to strive for… Until a year later, I started going to church and I became friends with the Proshak family. They started to take me to stay with their family on the weekends and I began to feel something. I felt as if I was needed somewhere. That feeling that I had, the feeling of darkness, was disappearing little by little. Now that I think about it, the definition of orphanage has not changed. It's still a world of darkness, but my attitude changed. Now, I have a sense of family; I am surrounded by a family environment. The definition of the orphanage did not change but my understanding of what was happening in my life changed because now I have a family of my own. I look at it in a different light, and I see as if I had to grow through it all to see how thankful I am for what I have now or even had at the time. Because if it wasn't for everything that happened to me at the orphanage, and I didn't even have it that bad because some of the students got beaten and bullied and, I was just lonely. If it weren't for the circumstances that I had to go through and live through, I wouldn't be the person I am today".*

Masha Krasovskaya, who is my dearest friend from the orphanage, someone who never got a chance to leave the orphanage. Masha graduated from the 11th grade, and you could say that Masha has seen it all. This is what an orphanage means to Masha:

"The orphanage means to me not a really happy childhood. I was at the orphanage since I was in the first grade, literally since 6 years old. And, outside of the nice travels between America and Italy, I would consider an orphanage to be a jail. When I arrived at the orphanage, I thought I would be there for a brief period of time, which clearly wasn't true, but right now, I think that the orphanage has made me a strong and independent woman. I was always on the move, I always thought that the orphanage wouldn't be a long stay for me, and I knew from the start that my mother wouldn't come get me. The reason why I thought my mother wouldn't come and get me was because I didn't even know her. Even now, I have no idea who she is or where she is; all I know is that her name is Lena and that she passed along some of her bad habits to me. When I think back on it, I think the orphanage has made me strong because even from the start, when I was in the 1st grade, I started to show my attitude to show my true self. I started to talk back, and the teachers did not like that, so I started to get beat up".

Lastly, this is what orphanage meant to someone who had never lived there, to an outsider who was still a part of our lives. Valentina Proshak, the oldest daughter of Nikolai and Anna Proshak. Valentina states that the orphanage is:

"The first thing that comes to my mind when I hear the word orphanage is actually an image. The image is from the Matveevskie orphanage, specifically the monument right in front of the school along with the huge building in the back

and the trees near it. It's the first thing you notice when you pull in. But if I did not know about the Matveevskie orphanage or how it looked, I would say that the orphanage is a place that is completely closed, where the kids dream about getting out, aging out and graduating. Just to be somewhere else and not at the orphanage. Also makes me think that the orphanage is always filled with lots of active kids. I say that because every time I visited, the kids were always on the move, and it seemed like they always had somewhere to be, as if they were late. They were always running".

The orphanage could mean home to many. A comfort zone that no matter where the kids came from, we all had related stories, similar backgrounds, and similar family situations. That you didn't have to be ashamed of yourself because there were others like you. Lots of others like you. The orphanage could mean nights of crying, waiting for your family member to pick you up. For those who have nobody, it is more difficult because they just want to end it: to run away and hide from everyone and everything. For some, an orphanage means a lot of waiting. Waiting for a day to end so you could be a day closer to aging out so they could leave. Waiting for someone to take you in, someone to adopt you. Waiting for a Friday night so you could take a bus to your hometown so you could spend the weekend with your aunt or grandparents.

Some teenagers can't wait to age, leave the orphanage, "Start a new life," as many would say. From my point of view, leaving the orphanage, knowing you are on your own and no one has your back when needed, is scary. Teenagers who have less or no power at all are destroyed. Whose life gets ruined over something that their parents did ages ago. They get destroyed not only physically but mentally as well. They get beat up by those who have the power to take their monthly pension checks away. By leaving others with no money to live on, so they steal. Steal from the roommates - get caught, get beat up, lose trust of those around. Life's purpose just ended right there. No money, no people who trust you, no family to go to. For girls, it's even worse. Can you imagine yourself leaving the orphanage after the 9th or 11th grade and getting pregnant? To have no one to turn to and ask for help or simple advice. That's one of those moments when you think that life isn't fair. Beginning of questioning why is God putting you through that? Why did your parents leave you just like that? Asking yourself if you are worth it? I can't picture myself getting older and getting pregnant at the age of 18. Even though I had people who had my back in the situations, I was feeling down, empty inside, and blaming myself for everything that had happened to me. My life was difficult if I hadn't had those people there for me when I needed a shoulder to cry on - it would've been so much harder than it already was. I was one of the lucky ones!

Once I got used to the whole orphanage life, which basically meant if I saw something that I shouldn't, no I didn't. I kept my head down as much as I could and didn't ask any questions. One day, my only friend Anya told me all about her Sundays and that she would go to church.

"Church???" I remember asking with a shock on my face. She told me that there's a man who would pick up a certain number of kids and would take them to his church. Afterward, he would take them downtown to do something fun. A couple of days later, I met this guy, and he invited me to come to his church the next Sunday. I agreed. I thought I could check it out, knowing I had nothing better to do on Sundays. I also had never been to an actual church before, so I had no idea what to expect. My family wasn't Christian, but I knew that there was God. However, knowing God and believing in God are different. Sunday came, and I was ready to go.

I wore the only pair of jeans that I owned and some ugly sweater. Since it was around November, as every day went by, it was getting chiller outside. There were around ten of us who went to church that day. The name of the man who picked us up was Nicolia Valentinovich. He drove a white Mercedes Benz; in Ukraine, people would call it a Marshrutka (Minibus). As he picked us up, my friend Anya and I sat in the back, and let me tell you this: the second I got into that car, I knew from the beginning that I didn't belong there. The way I was dressed, the way I talked, the way I represented myself, it was the feeling that I fell to the ground from a whole other planet. Also, who knew that the service would be two hours? I was not prepared for that at all.

It was a Baptist Church where men wore fancy suits, and women wore long skirts and fancy tops. I was falling asleep —no joke. After the service, people would give me "Welcome" and "So happy to meet you" hugs. I felt uncomfortable just because I didn't know who those people were and where I was, yet even though I didn't know where I was or who the men were who brought us to church, I didn't want to go back to the orphanage. Something was holding me back, and at the time, I had no idea who it was or what it was. It felt so warm. Nikolai Valentinovich introduced me to his family: a beautiful wife with three gorgeous daughters. His older daughter Valya and I found contact quickly - months later, we became best friends who shared memories and inside jokes.

After that one Sunday, I couldn't wait for another one and then the one after that. I felt connected with those people in many ways. I couldn't get connected with people at the orphanage. After the service, Nicolai Valentinovich would try to come up with a plan for us to do something fun - instead of just dropping us off at the orphanage. It would be rides to McDonald's (There's only one McDonald's in the city of Zaporizhzhia - the city's population is 746,749). Get ice cream or sunflower seeds and go for a long walk in the local park if the weather is nice. Even staying at the church, cooking our own dinner, and playing mafia afterward is way better than returning to the orphanage life, but worse food.

I was getting closer and closer as every week went by. Strangers turned into people who I would call a family. I began to get more involved with the orphanage because of Nikolai Valentinovich. Some days after school, he would come over and teach driver's ed to students, and some days, he would bring over some bikes and let us bike around in the soccer field. We would all take turns after rounds. I remember laughing and having an enjoyable time, having not a single sad nerve in my body, just pure joy. Spending Sundays with Nikolai Valentinovich's world was turning into picking us up on Friday after school and bringing us back to the orphanage on Monday morning before school.

The Proshak family was basically my family, and they took me in. Now, if I could say their last name aloud, it would put a smile on my face because I only have good memories of spending time with that family. I remember my first New Year at the orphanage. I was supposed to spend the Holiday with the Proshak family, but I had a cold, so I had to stay at the orphanage to avoid getting anyone sick. However, when the sickness went away, I came over for the weekend, and they still had a fake Christmas tree and a lot of chocolate waiting for me under the tree. Just the thought that they took time to get me something, that they thought of me in the first place, meant the whole world to me. I felt loved and belonged.

In January 2012, the American organization OHHC (Open Hearts and Homes for Children) came to interview orphans at my orphanage. I remember being called to the Director's office, and the whole class was, "Kristina what did you do this time?" I had no idea what was happening. The second I walked in, I saw two men; one of them looked scarier than the other. They introduced themselves. The translator told me and the others who got a chance to get interviewed that if we got lucky, we would have an opportunity to go to the United States.

"United States?" I couldn't believe what I was hearing. "As in America? As in, Obama is the president? "As in New York, like in movies?" I couldn't stop asking questions, the translator couldn't stop smiling, and my director was giving me looks - letting me know that I should sit still and be quiet. That's what I did. I couldn't stop thinking about it because I knew there was no way I could be the one who'd get picked. I knew that I wasn't that lucky, I knew I wasn't special and wasn't any different than the rest of 300 children at the orphanage.

The translator began to ask me questions, such as "What's your favorite food?" "Do you like pets?" "What is your favorite thing to do in your free time?" and so on. I remember one question the translator asked me: "Who do you want to become in the future?" I wanted to say a cashier because my aunt was a cashier and she always wanted to own her own store, but the director said "Kristina, stop being a clown and say something serious" I said I would love to be a lawyer one day. Why lawyer? Hearing the life about the orphanage on TV and actually living it and experiencing it is very different. I always wanted to do something about it. Starting with the laws in the surrounding community.

Yet, here I am, trying to be a writer? Time flies faster than it should. Not even a month later, five other students and I were called down to see the director. None of us knew what was happening, and we were asking each other, "What did you do?" When in reality, none of us had done anything wrong. As we walked into her office, Larissa Konstantinovna told us to take a seat; we all were nervous and were freaking out- not knowing what to expect; we all sat down.

"One mistake, and I will call your families to let them know you can't go. I am going to watch every step of yours, making sure you do what your teachers and caretakers ask you to. Do you hear me? One mistake! You can go now." We didn't move. One of the girls decided to ask:

"What's going on?" - The director took her eyes off the documents she was working on.

"The five of you were chosen to go to the United States for the summer. Marina Konstantinovna is going to be your supervisor.

I believe for one second my heart just **STOPPED**.

Every time I left Larissa's Kanstantinovna office, I would stop and stare. As I stared, I would take my time... right out of her office to the left of her door; she had this board of awareness pretty much. On that board, it was about twenty of the best students known to be good at something. There were students who were good at gymnastics, boxing, drawing, Champions who brought the orphanage fame by having the best grades and winning medals by completing other schools. I mean the list went on. And every time I would walk by the board I would stop and stare because I knew I had nothing in me. My soul was empty. I had absolutely nothing special in me that would get me my picture on that wall. A picture on the wall that would get me respect from anyone. I was average. I wasn't good at school, and the teachers weren't trying to go above and beyond to make us super smart; they were just doing their jobs. I wasn't good at art, dancing, sewing, ceramics, or sports. I was average. I knew nothing would get me on that board because that would mean replacing one of those students' photos with mine. I was average. And here I was… getting ready to take over America.

CHAPTER 5

BEING ABLE TO LIVE AND NOT EXIST

"Next week, the six of you are going to Kyiv to get a visa." - we all exchanged massive looks. Two of the girls who were chosen to go to the United States had been overseas before. When I told my grandmother and my aunt I was chosen, they were against it! Especially my aunt, she thought that my host family would sell my body parts to get extra cash. I couldn't listen to her nonsense anymore, so I did not stay in touch with my biological family until I came back to Ukraine.

When visas and the documents were ready, we hit the road. In total, there were six of us, five kids and the supervisor. We took an overnight train to the capital of Ukraine, Kyiv, where we met up with kids from all over the country. At the airport, the supervisors made us wear bright yellow T-shirts so we all could stay together as a group and have less chance of losing or leaving someone behind. Picture this: over one hundred children wearing bright T-shirts, so bright your eyes hurt. You'd most likely ask questions. All of this was new to me: the people, the T-shirts, having a visa, being at the airport and hearing languages other than Russian and Ukrainian. I was confused and didn't know how to react to it. Most of the kids were losing excitement. I felt weird. Then I looked around and realized that I wasn't alone. I wasn't the only one who was at the airport for the first time. I wasn't the only one who was leaving the country for the first time. I wasn't the only one who had never flown on an airplane before. It made me feel better; I smiled. Even though I had no idea what to expect and what exactly I was putting myself into. Yet, what I did know was that no one was going to sell my body parts.

Location: Kievs airport. We all wore neon bright yellow "Open Hearts & Homes" t-shirts; to easily locate our group, in-case we got lost.

The first flight wasn't bad at all. It was only three hours if I remember correctly. We flew from Kyiv, Ukraine to Frankfurt, Germany. Once we got to Germany people were speaking either German or English. I couldn't understand or speak either. I had no idea what was happening around me. I had time to look around and experience the feeling of being somewhere where people had no idea who I was, where I was from or where I was going. That's where it all begins feeling more real. All the supervisors were screaming as loud as they could, "Stay together," "Do not get lost," and "Don't lose your ticket or passport unless you want to spend your summer alone in Germany." People around me were tall, with serious facial expressions, and well-dressed. I couldn't help but stare. I wondered what people thought of seeing all of us dressed the same, who didn't look like they fit in, or who knew their native language. The airport was bigger and fancier than the one in Kyiv. Once we got to the security, it was scarier; even though I had nothing illegal on me, we didn't know what to expect. The workers carefully went through our stuff, ensuring we were clean. Luckily for us, we got to the plane with no issues.

Once we got onto the second plane, the supervisors handed us letters from our host families. In the letters, families would talk about how they were excited to meet us and spend most of the summer together. Once I got my letter, I felt nothing but warmth. The letter was so colorful, full of a bunch of pictures, yet more importantly, the letter was in perfect Russian. I was surprised. The second I read my letter, I found out that two of the host siblings had been adopted from Ukraine. I couldn't be more excited to meet them and to hear their story. The airplane ride was way longer than all of us expected. Eleven hours in the air is a bit extreme, don't you think? My ears started popping, and I couldn't hear anything around me. I didn't know how to react to it or how to make it go away. I was scared. I cried. The thought that I would have to do the exact same thing on the way home did not make me happy. I was over it. As you read it, I did not enjoy my first experience flying - in other words, it was a nightmare.

When we landed, I didn't know where to look or what to look for. The most important thing that stood out to me was how comfortable people were with just being themselves. I saw families sitting on the floor and casually eating dinner, taking a quick nap right next to the trash can. No one cared if your shoes were Nike or from a local thrift shop. Above all, the airport was overflowing with genuine families who were just as nervous as we were. To me, it practically looked as if I was in the zoo; it was so different from my country. I remember feeling some type of way, an unexplainable feeling that I will never forget. Seeing many children reuniting with their host families gave me a warm feeling. A feeling I won't ever be able to forget because I was there. I was one of those host children who got a really warm welcoming with giant posters, stuffed animals and love - almost too good to be true. While I was just exploring and walking through the airport, seeing my now friends meeting their host families, I met Kevin. The American who came to my orphanage gave me a big welcome hug. As he hugged me, he said something unfamiliar, and we started walking, which now I assume was "Common". It was nice to see someone somewhat familiar. As we slowly walked, my heart dropped. I didn't know what to say. I forgot how to breathe. Kevin walked me to a family member who was holding a poster with MY picture on it. It was odd to see myself with really short hair on the poster, where I almost looked too sad to be alive. It was a big family who gave me so many hugs and welcomed me with nice smiles. It was Kevin's family. Most of them looked familiar from the family letters they gave us on the airplane. Not going to lie; I felt pretty fancy spending my summer in the United States with the person who came to my orphanage. However, deep down, it was also terrifying; I didn't want to give Kevin and his family the wrong impression of me. I was scared that if I said something wrong or if, they would send me back or, worse, call my director at the orphanage and tell her how awful I was. She was a really intelligent woman but when needed to be she could be a scary one, too.

Summer 2012 – My sister Oksana and I enjoying a late night face mask.

    Since Kevin and Aileen were a part of the organization that allowed me and other children to come to America, they had to make sure that every single child got reunited with their host family and was safe and sound. Since there were a couple of families who had to take a morning flight home we had to spend the night at the nearest hotel. The next morning, we had to make sure that the families got on the plane with no issues. After which we hit the road... The state the Clay family was living in was New Hampshire; the drive from New York was about four hours long. I was sort of lamed out that I had never heard of a state such as New Hampshire. Most of my friends were staying in states like Virginia, North Carolina, Washington, or New York. Even when I was telling other kids from the program where I would be living for the next month, they would raise their eyebrows and say, "Where???" "How do you pronounce that??" However, I did get lucky with having a sister and a brother who were both adopted from Ukraine and who were also speaking Russian. It was a big bonus and came in handy because it seemed like the whole stay, I had my personal translator.

The month in America flew faster than I imagined. Yet, adjusting was harder than I pictured. I didn't eat anything besides fruits and vegetables and slept at funny times such as right after dinner time or in the back seat coming home after a dinner out. During that whole month, my host mom, Aileen, didn't give me a chance to ever be bored; she made sure I had something to do on a daily basis. We either went for a drive to run her errands, went to the pool, waterpark, roller coasters, painted pottery, or just as simple as having a family night and watching movies.

One evening, Aileen asked me if I wanted to come for a ride with her and my host sister, Oksana. I remember how freaked out I was when my host sister sat behind the wheel and started the car, and I remember asking her, "Is this legal?", she would laugh at me and shake her head as yes. The point is that my host mom was actually worried about me. She took her time to make sure I was having fun and making unforgettable memories in the country that I could possibly never come back to. The family I could possibly never come back to. Within a month, I felt comfortable calling Aileen and Kevin's mother and father, of course, with their permission. Yet, there were moments that brought me a step back and awoke me. The fact that those people weren't my actual parents and their children weren't my actual siblings. One night, my fairytale was over. We all were celebrating Kevin's birthday, and I was so excited for him to read the card that I had picked out for him myself. Even though I only understood half of what the card was saying, what is so memorable about that evening is that every sibling wrote "Father" or "Dad" on the envelope. So, did I. I wrote "DAD" with big fat letters. Yet, then I was pulled aside and told to erase and say "Kevin" instead, since he wasn't actually my Dad. It was a realization that I was just a stranger, and I was blessed to be here for a good time and not a long time. It was an "Oh shit" moment that made me take a step back and hide in the corner to not make everyone else uncomfortable for trying to steal someone else's spotlight and, importantly, their Dad.

Mid-way through my stay, my supervisor, Marina Kanstantinovna, came to visit me and spent a few nights. It was really nice to see a familiar face. Aileen took us to amusement parks and other fun places to ensure Marina had an awesome stay, but importantly, to let my director know that I am safe and doing great.

Every day, no matter where I went or who I went with, you'd find Oksana walking around with a camera around her neck. Photographing every little thing I did making me feel like a celebrity who had their own paparazzi. To which she'd respond, "Before you leave, we're going to print them out, and you can take them with you and show everyone how your stay went," as she would smile and take another photo. There were nights when Aileen, Oksana and I just baked muffins and cupcakes at midnight while everyone was already in bed. Then, the next morning, we'd have them at breakfast, and Kevin would ask, "Where did those come from?" and the three of us wouldn't say anything yet; instead, we would exchange looks and smiles, making everything pretty obvious.

Celebrating the 4th of July was unforgettable, truly better than just seeing the parade on the TV. People who were in the parade didn't matter if they were driving or walking; they were all still so happy and genuine. We all were sitting on the grass celebrating the holiday, right next to the parents, who were sitting in those fancy, relaxing chairs. People who were in the parade began to throw candy at us. I was confused. I'll tell you that. Once I turned around, I saw other kids picking the candy off the ground as if they were in "Hunger Games" and fighting for their lives. I was no different from them. I got up and began to collect any candy that I could find near me. As I did so, I heard more than laugh; my foster brothers were laughing and giggling at me. They even began to point fingers at me and the little kids next to us. Pretty much saying that I am a "child," but that didn't stop me. Why should I be ashamed of myself for picking up lollipops that were pretty much given to me? After the parade, Kevin and Aileen took all of us to the center of our village. We heard different bands playing and speeches, and saw many cute dogs and little animals. Many people were selling baked goods, popcorn and even caramel apples? I have never heard of such a thing. To me, it just doesn't look that good? (No offense). It wasn't until years later that I tried a caramel apple, and let me tell you… why no one convinced me to try them sooner?!!! Afterwards, we went to the local high school to watch the fireworks. I met a lot of Oksana's friends and teachers, and almost everyone knew me. I guess I was pretty popular.

It was hard to think about leaving because I got so attached to my host sister, Oksana; even though we were different ages, we had a lot in common. Orphanage and the life before it. We spent nights talking about our lives, the reasons why we ended up in the orphanage and our families. I felt like she was my soulmate. That was when I deeply wished I had an older sister like Oksana. Even though I've only spent a month with this family, I'd built such strong connections with them. Different sorts of connections with everyone individually. It was a heart-warming connection.

Once the day came to say goodbye, I wasn't ready. I looked ready, but deep down, I knew I wasn't. How can I just leave everyone and everything and be okay with it? Saying goodbyes is always hard. I especially did not know how I was going to say goodbye to my new best friend, Oksana. Once we arrived at the airport and it was for real that time… The time to hug goodbye, the time to cry and wave as I walked closer to my group and my friends and farther away from the family who made me feel that I was enough. Yet, that wasn't the case. Once we arrived at the airport, The Clay family checked in, and they all sat down. For a moment, I thought we were doing that for good luck. In Ukraine, there is a tradition where before traveling far, people sit down and sit in silence for a few minutes for good luck, as I said. Although, once we sat down, Kevin stood up and said something in English to Oksana, and then she looked at me and said.

"Mom and Dad have something to say to you, and I am going to translate," she smiled.

My heart dropped. This is it. I am in trouble and before I go, they will yell at me and tell me how terrible I was and never want to see me again… As Oksana was translating, my soul left the body. I wasn't present. I was so nervous, I couldn't stop biting my lip and my leg was bouncing up and down nonstop. Just like that, I was brought back to earth; I said, "What?"I couldn't believe my ears. The room was spinning. "We would like you to become a part of our family," Oksana translated.

No way, I thought. I was wanted. Kevin and Aileen wanted ME to be their daughter. I began to tear up, but those tears weren't sad tears; they were tears of joy and happiness. Now, I can fly back to my homeland with peace in my heart because I know that across the whole world, there is someone who wants me in their life. And, importantly, I needed them more. As we were saying another goodbye, my name was called by my supervisor, Maria Kanstantinovna. It was time to go for real now. I waved my last goodbye and slowly walked deeper into the airport until I couldn't see the

Clay family anymore. Once the group supervisors found our gate, they gave us our passports, and as always, they screamed, "Do not lose your passports unless you want to spend the night at the airport all by yourself." That wouldn't be too terrible, I thought to myself.

While we all waited at the gate, my friends and I were showing each other what cool stuff our host families got for us over the summer. Believe it or not, there was some trading going on. The supervisors were not too happy about that. They told us to be thankful for what we had and, if we didn't like it, to suck it up because there were many kids back home at the orphanage who would take it all within seconds. Wouldn't even think twice about it. The truth is they all were right; at that moment, we looked very ungrateful. But it was just stuff. Stuff that I have never owned before, stuff that I have never seen in my life before. Yet, for some reason, it didn't matter to me. Because even though I was a "poor" child whose life was all fucked up, and I may have had the coolest shoes and the brightest shocks on, I didn't care. What I did care about was the thought that I couldn't stop thinking about. I couldn't stop picturing in my head when I was going to see my family again. That's what made me feel alive.

CHAPTER 6
SUMMER CAMP AS AN ORPHAN

After we safely returned to our homeland, the bus from our orphanage picked us up. It was hard to say another goodbye to all the new friends I made from other orphanages who were in the same program as me. We told each other "Hope to see you again." I did have a phone; it was a Samsung that was falling apart. When I say it was falling apart, I mean it. The back battery was falling out, so the only solution was to tape the battery to the phone, which would work until the tape would get old and simply untaped itself from the phone. I did lose the battery a few times on the campus of the orphanage and searching for it was not fun, I'll tell you that. The phone itself was not a touchscreen, and since it was an INCREDIBLY old phone, I couldn't even see the keyboard and the letters on the keyboard were washed away, you could say. Sometimes, to text, I would have to play a guessing game to guess where the letter L is and where the letter D is. To type something in English, like a password to a platform, was absolutely impossible. Since the letters were washed away, guessing where the letters were would take even longer because I didn't know the English alphabet. Not that I know it now… But my new friends and I exchanged social media, and we just all hoped for the best. We hoped to see each other again.

On the way to the orphanage, I, of course, shared the good news of me getting adopted; everyone was really happy for me. What's even more special is the fact that almost everyone asked to be adopted. Riding home was weird. What's more bizarre is calling the orphanage "home."

What's even more bizarre is the fact that some kids grew up not knowing or having another home other than the orphanage...

Riding on that bus made me realize something. Before this trip overseas, I had never been friends with those kids who came. I never got along with some boys who came, and even older girls like Lena. She was older; therefore, she had no interest in being my friend. Yet, this new experience that we all shared, where we all had common stories, brought us closer. Now we were all friends, and that made me happy. It made me happy because this trip made a human out of me. After all, now I was no longer a loser who owned one pair of jeans. Who had holes in socks, and didn't know how to properly dress herself.

As we arrived at the orphanage, our director, Larissa Kanstantinovna, was waiting for us at the front door. Even though she may seem like a scary lady who would bite me in my sleep if I ran in the halls and not walk slowly, I still missed her. It was one of those "It's good to be home" moments. She gave each and every one of us a warm hug and a kiss and told us that we had packages waiting for us in our rooms. The packages included what we were supposed to bring with us for a month at the summer camp on the Black Sea. Every summer, the orphanage would get coupons to take all of the kids who had nowhere to go to camp. The camp was strictly for orphanage kids. I was told that to keep everyone on campus was too expensive. This way, we all could take a break from the orphanage and get some sun and it's a great opportunity to meet new people from different towns. Plus, the supervisors do deserve a break from all of us.

As that sentence was said, all of the girls exchanged a disgusted look. Meaning, "Ew, we're going to wear the exact same clothes that the orphanage provided for every single girl." After a good minute of begging the director and her sister, if we could just bring the clothes the American families provided for us, they gave up. They told us that if something goes missing or someone steals something, we should not come to them and cry on their shoulders because they would tell us, "I told you so."

It was six of us kids and a new super supervisor, Valentina N. I never liked her, she was too strict and I guess "too by the book." Every time something would happen to me at the orphanage, like someone stealing my shoes, she would blame me for being too stupid and giving someone an opportunity to take them. I guess she was right, but she never wanted to help. I guess she had seen enough of shit going on at the orphanage that, at that point, every news seemed too old for her to deal with, so she just gave up. And I probably would too if I was in her position, but after understanding her side, I still didn't like her.

The ride from the orphanage to the summer camp was about two hours, which seemed too long at the moment. I couldn't wait any longer to see my friends, and I was also too excited to give everyone the gifts that my host mom bought for everyone. When we arrived, I felt "famous" in a way; everyone was running up to us and asking who we were and what orphanage we were from. We had a small group of kids, but to the outsiders, we looked like a small family who rolled up like "tough" people. Some people found us tough-looking because we all stocked together, and I don't blame them.

This was the first camp that I had ever been to as an orphan. I had no idea what to expect, and honestly, being at the all orphan's summer camp kind of gave me chills. I had no idea what was going to come out of this. Considering the fact that there were teenagers from orphanages that are also mental facilities. As we arrived, our camp counselor brought us to the building where we were staying. At this camp, each building number was based on the grade. But since we arrived at the midpoint of the summer, we have had a mix and match of both older and younger kids. A mix and match from different orphanages. Our two supervisors were two brothers who were obsessed with their bodies and working out. But at the same time, they didn't really care about what we did or what time we came back to the dorms. They kept saying they didn't get paid enough to care about every little detail that we did. Their advice was not to get caught because if we did get caught, they would actually have to punish us, and that was something that no one wanted.

You would think that after we arrived people would think we are "special" in the way, but no. People didn't care to ask what were our names and such. There was barely any room in the building that was provided for us. When the girls and I got assigned to different rooms, girls who already lived there judged us because we were in their "territory." I for sure didn't feel like the bedroom I was sleeping in was my safe place because it wasn't. Had to sleep with one eye open for safety reasons. I felt like I was too late to the game because, at that point, everyone already knew everyone. It was awkward to walk around and ask everyone, "What is your name?" People would've just laughed. The majority of the kids I lived with were from the Zaporozhie orphanage. There was one orphanage that didn't have the best reputation, and I have heard some stuff about that place, which is not really good like stealing, drugs and fights. Kids literally going crazy. That kind of stuff had also happened at my orphanage, but I knew everyone and I guess knew their reasons too. With these kids? I didn't know them, so I guess it was easier to judge them than to get to know them.

As I settled in, I went to the bleachers and took a deep breath. I looked around to see if I was alone, and I was.

I took out my phone, which was barely holding together and dialed in a phone number that I used to remember by heart. Soon enough, I heard a "Hello", from another line. My heart was beating so freaking fast, and at that moment, I felt like I forgot how to speak.

"Hello?"

"Hi grandmother, it's Kristina," I said. My body was covered in goosebumps, the little hairs on my arms were standing up, I was so nervous.

"Kristina??? Inna, come over here Kristina is on the phone. Where have you been? It's been months since you called us. Are you okay?" My aunt and my grandmother had so many questions for me, and I wasn't sure how I was supposed to answer them all and be put together. After taking many deep breaths, I told them that I had come back from my trip to America. They, of course, asked me if I got beaten and if they were nice to me. I didn't have enough balls to tell them at that particular moment that I was getting adopted overseas. My grandmother had heart problems, and I knew this would cause her pain, so I didn't. I was also afraid that they wouldn't approve. I knew exactly who and how my family was, and this news wasn't for them to hear.

Spending the rest of my summer at the summer camp on the Black Sea wasn't too terrible. I got a chance to meet new people from other orphanages and sooner or later, I had my own group of people who I did everything with. Every night, the leader of the whole camp would give every group an assignment where we would come up with something as a group, like a contest. Every assignment differed from one another, like dancing, singing, mimicking someone or something, or coming up with a play. After dinner, we would all get together for those camp activities where each group would show everyone what they came up with. At the end of the event, the camp leader would announce the group who won and of course, deliver a present. Something for the whole group, like pizza or a stuffed animal for everyone individually. After the event, the DJ would announce "Discoteka", which was everyone's favorite. Of course, based on the group you were in that determines how long you could stay at the discoteka. My group was old enough to stay till the discoteka was over, which most of the time would end at 11 P.M. Every camp that I have been to almost had the same schedule to follow on a daily basis. The older I got, the more flexible the supervisors have gotten:

- 8 A.M. – wake up
- 8:15 A.M.– stretching time
- 8:30 A.M – cleaning the dorms
- 9 A.M – breakfast
- 10 A.M-1 P.M– group activities
- 1 P.M-1:30 P.M – free time (at this time, we were allowed to go off campus to go to the market and get junk food)
- 1:30 P.M – lunch
- 2 P.M-3:30 P.M – afternoon nap
- 3:30 P.M – afternoon snack
- 4 P.M-6 P.M – group activities
- 6 P.M-7 P.M – free time
- 7 P.M – dinner
- 8 P.M – camp activities
- 9:30 P.M– 11 P.M ish diskoteka
- 11 P.M – second dinner
- 11:30 P.M – bedtime.

If you were older, you were allowed to skip most of the stuff on the daily schedule, which allowed me to have more free time. My supervisors didn't care enough to follow the schedule strictly; the only thing that was on the schedule that we as a group, took really seriously was, of course, going to the dining hall on time. The dining hall wasn't big enough for all of the group on the campsite to eat at the same time. So, the older the group was, the later they would eat. Afternoon snacks and second dinner were my favorite meals at the camp. This is something that we didn't have to go to the dining hall; the supervisors would have to go to the dining hall to pick it up and give it out at an appropriate time. An afternoon snack would be something like fruits, cookies and candy. A second dinner would look like ice cream or some type of pastry and a juicy box. The second favorite thing I did care about on the schedule was group activities after breakfast. This meant we all went to the beach.

Most of the girls would tan at the beach, and the boys would have swimming competitions or water fights. And then there was me, a weirdo who would collect shells. By doing so, I definitely got made fun of, but I was too deep into collecting shells to care. Every half an hour, a person would walk by the beach screaming, "Dried fish, corn on the cob, beer," and every half hour repeat. If you would drive on the Main Street of the town, you would see outside of every house; there is a small store in the front yard. A couple of small tables and a few giant signs saying, "FreshDried Fish." A house after house, a table after table, a sign after another. Just writing about it reminds me how watery my mouth was because that was one of the times I wished I had money to buy all the dried fish there was.

Not too far away from our beach site, there was a giant water slide that led straight into the sea. I think to go down, it was like 10 Grivnas; the boys from our group always would sneak away to go down the water slide. There was also a giant banana ride. Where it's almost like a jet ski, but in this case, it was a banana. About three to four people could fit on it, and the only thing you could hold onto were these tiny black handles on the side of the banana. The banana would circle around, allowing people to fall off it, which was the best part. I never went on it because I never had money again, but I heard it from people who did go there. Once in a while, we would have sand competitions, where each group had to build something out of sand in a given time. Many groups took this competition seriously, and of course, there were other groups who tried to sabotage everyone's work just so they could win, which was very typical.

Showers at the camp were in another building outside of the building where we lived. There were two separate shower cabins, one for boys and one for girls. The shower cabins had about twenty shower heads, with no walls or curtains separating from one another. Privacy cost money, money that we didn't have; therefore, we had to use what was provided for us. Girls had to take showers with bathing suits on, but even then, we had to be careful. The roof had holes that were big enough for the boys to spy on us. There were days when the shower cabins didn't have enough hot water or any water at all. Some choose not to shower or to shower in the boy's cabins.

One sizzling summer day, my friends and I had big plans for the night. Since there was a discoteka every night, we all must look nice, and being clean was part of it. My friend Yulia thought that she was going to get asked out; as her friends, we all must be there for her to support her and all that. Of course, that particular day, the shower cabins had no water in them at all, and we didn't feel comfortable showering at the boy's cabin. So, what we did instead was actually pretty fun and smart, in my opinion. We took our shower supplies and headed to the sea; there weren't many people at the beach, which we thought was good because we didn't want to get judged. Showering at the sea was one of the best memories that I remember sharing with my friends at that summer camp. We all were laughing as we were covered in shampoo foam all over our bodies. Now, thinking back on it, we most definitely looked super ridiculous.

After our little adventure, we of course got into trouble. : Families at the beach told the camp's director on us. They said that it was really disturbing to watch, that it was a really bad example to their kids, and that they were not aware of what was happening at the camp. The first people who got the first punch were our supervisors; afterwards, they screamed at us pretty much to the point where we were crying. They also screamed at us in front of everyone and didn't even bother to call us aside. After that, we looked bad in front of everyone in our group. The punishment that we received wasn't just for my friends and I; it was for the whole group. We weren't allowed to be present at the discoteka. You can imagine what kind of issues this caused. Of course, there were girls who didn't even bother to listen but instead decided to sneak out, saying they were too pretty to sit in the dorm all night. You could also imagine how upset my friend Yulia was, but that feeling went away shortly after her Prince Charming climbed the tree that led right into our dorm.

There was this girl Jasmira, from my orphanage. She was in a different camp group, but after I had just arrived at the camp, the first thing she did was compliment my shoes. She said something about the brand being really rare in Ukraine and how it's almost impossible to find them locally. I, of course, felt fancy because those were the shoes that my host mother bought for me in America. Jasmira was known for being a bully at my orphanage, where no one even wanted to breathe near her. She was a savage because if she didn't get what she wanted, she wasn't afraid to throw hands. One time at the orphanage, every Friday, our director allowed students to go home for the weekend after signing a few forms. Jasmira had a grandmother who lived in Zaporizhzhia, about half an hour away from the orphanage. After her grandmother passed away, she had no one to visit, but she didn't say anything about her grandmother passing away to our director, Larissa Kanstantinovna.

One Friday, she went to ask her class leader to sign her form, but she said no because, at this point, the word of her grandmother's passing spread around. After hearing "no", Jasmira hit her class leader. So you see, after she complimented my shoes and I said "thank you," but I knew that she was up to something fishy.

Few days into my being at the camp, Jasmira came to see me at my dorm. She came to see if she could borrow the shoes for the diskoteka that night. I felt like I was in a position where I couldn't say no. Jasmira left with my shoes in her hand and a smile on her face, saying that she would take good care of them for me. I was nervous. After that a few days went by, and I sort of forgot that I let Jasmira barrow my shoes; it wasn't until I saw her wearing them to the dining hall that I remembered. I came up to her and told her that after lunch, I'm going to stop by her dorm to pick them up. She smirked. When I showed up at her dorm, she wasn't there, and her roommates wouldn't let me go inside the dorm to look for the shoes. The next day, I saw Jasmira again, but this time she wasn't wearing the shoes. When I told her again that I would like my shoes back, she looked at me, made a really sad face and said that they got stolen. I panicked and started crying because how could I be so stupid and naïve to let her wear the shoes that were gifted to me by my host mom??

This was the moment where I wished I had listened to Larissa Kanstantinovna and should've left them at the orphanage, where they would've been under a lock. But no, I wanted to show off. As a few days went by, I saw Jasmira at the diskoteka wearing MY shoes. But this time, I didn't say anything to her directly. I told my supervisors that Jasmira stole my shoes and wouldn't give them back to me; the next day in my free time, he took me to see Jasmira. Once she saw me and my giant supervisor, she freaked out a bit. It was victory time. I came back to my dorm carrying my fancy shoes with me.

Towards the end of our stay at the camp, my friends and I realized that we had some little stuff that was missing. We had been borrowing each other's clothes and small girls' stuff like hairbrushes all the time. But once we came together, we realized that it was actually missing because neither of us had each other's stuff. We had our suspicions, but we knew if we would have pointed fingers, a War World III would start, so we stayed quiet. Soon enough, this conversation came up again, but this time, other girls were talking. At the same point, t-shirts and socks were missing. Another girl realized that she had let her friend borrow a bathing suit in the beginning of the camp, and she hasn't seen it since. After hearing so many girls complain that they had something missing, we all saw a pattern.

All of the girls whose stuff was missing were from my orphanage; not a single girl from Zaporozhie's orphanage spoke up about anything missing. We told one of our oldest and "strongest" not physically but mentally friend Lena, she was obviously from our orphanage. When we told her what was going on she and some other girls came over from their group. Meanwhile, most of the kids were at the beach. Lena and her friends began to scan and flip beds, and it was honestly so scary to see how angry they all were. I mean, we were too, because it was unfair. We weren't the rich kids from a gated community; we were united?! We were the same; the only thing that was different about us were our names... When Lena didn't find anything, we felt disgusted.

Disgusting for betraying our own. But that feeling went away quickly. One of Lena's friends didn't hesitate to push one of the closets aside. There we all were.

Surrounding what it felt like gold. The closet was hiding a hole in the wall, and in the hole, there were bag after bag full of clothes and small belongings like hair accessories and makeup. We dumped all of the bags out in the center of the floor, and like bad bitches we waited for them to come. It was honestly sad. Sad because they felt like they needed to steal from us, kids who didn't have much. That could mean one thing, that they didn't get this kind of stuff at their orphanage, so they had to find other ways on how to "survive." So a part of me understood why they did what was done. When a bunch of girls came inside the dorm and saw what was happening, they didn't say anything. They just sat down and started crying; I felt bad. Lena called everyone into those girls' dorm and told them to look through the pile and see if anything was theirs. Many people were in and out. And I can't even imagine what those girls felt at that particular moment. Was it shame??? Or what is disappointment? Disappointed because their mission failed?!

Overall, I do think that I had a great time at the summer camp as an orphan. I was glad to feel related in a way to every single person at the camp site; we all were there because our lives were shit. Even as individuals, we all were different people, but at the end of the day, we were at the same spot point in life. That's what united all of us as a whole. Saying goodbye to my new friends from the different orphanages was hard because we had no idea if there's going to be the next time. Seeing bus after bus full of orphan kids leave the camp site was sad. I think I even cried because this meant it was time for a reality check. It was time to go home.

CHAPTER 7

THE AMERICAN CHRISTMAS

The first Ukrainian crisis that I was aware occurred in November 2013. During most days, we'd watch - that i was aware of what was happening in Kyiv on TV as the whole grade. I remember being scared and, most importantly, being amazed about the fact that we were this close to war. We saw people dying. Dying due to peaceful protest, due to speaking about their truth. Due to calling out the government, calling out at the time President Viktor, because he fucked up big time. In November, Yanukovych rejected with European Union. Ukraine of course, was not happy, and people wanted to be heard, so they protested, and of course Europe and America supported the protesters, but Russia, on the other hand, supported the decision of the ex-president. Many were saying that somehow the president or the government got to peoples cell phones, so when so and so called each other and spoke on the phone about going to the Maidan to the protest, somehow those people would go missing… and somehow a peaceful protest turned into bloody protest full of violence and robbery. This was the night that the government robbed the civil citizens' voice.

This was happening until February, when, of course, the ex-president ran away. Can you guess where he ran away to? He ran to Russia, where Putin welcomed him with open arms. And of course, since then, shit went south and later on, Russia even took over Cremia and now a beautiful part of Ukraine where people would visit for summer vacations is now a part of Russia. It was definitely super scary seeing the things that we'd read in books happen in real life and, especially on TV or live. If you're interested in discovering more about what happened to Ukraine in 2013, please watch "Winter on Fire"— a documentary on Netflix that shows and covers what happened in Ukraine.

One visit overseas brought me popularity. Just like that, I was no longer that weird girl who owned one pair of pants or that girl who had holes in her socks. Or that girl who was afraid to ask a supervisor for more shampoo because now I had my own shampoo and even conditioner. I had socks in every color there possibly was. I had stuff that made me stand out, like hair conditioner, for example, or a nice winter coat. In a way, having all the nice things definitely put a target on my back because I'm sure some girls were hungry like a wolf in a lost forest to have the nice things that I had. Hungry for those socks and the hair conditioner. Because I had something that others didn't, girls from the upper class paid attention to me. It made me feel like I was being acknowledged as a human being. But the sad part about it is the fact that it took some useless things for people to SEE me.

There were still so many other people who deserved to be treated as human beings because they were one, but instead, because they had nothing to offer, they were automatically anything but time-consuming creators. Those people had to fight even harder to just have a normal day where no one would bully them and where they could have one night of sleep without being scared that someone is going to beat them up. I was one of those people, and one trip to America made everyone think that all of a sudden, I was the queen of England because on my feet were Nike shoes.

The boys from my grade finally saw me. I don't think they saw me for who I truly was, but at least now they acknowledged my presence and referred to me as "Kristina."

THE AMERICAN CHRISTMAS

Larissa Konstantinovna was also watching every single move of mine. Of course, everyone knew I was getting adopted, so with every assignment I was told to do, all of the teachers and supervisors added at the end of a sentence, "Do it right this time, or I will call your American family and tell them how awful you are so they will change their mind." At first, I thought it was funny and cute or whatever, but after a while, it got on my nerves. I knew they wouldn't actually call my "American family" as they stated. First of all, they couldn't afford to call America. Second of all, they cared too much, so they wouldn't dare to sabotage my future. No matter how much they actually hated me with all of their heart, at the end of the day, they wanted the best for each and every single one of us. I mean, it was actually their goal to make us successful!

After arriving back at the orphanage from my visit to America, every Saturday was special. The Clay family would call me every single Saturday after dinner time. It was one of the best feelings that I have ever experienced in my entire life. The conversation would go something like, "Hi, how are you?" "I'm good, how are you?" That's it. That's as far as my English skills went at the time. After that, I would ask for my sister Oksana to come to the phone. I would tell her everything, and she would translate for the rest of the family. I felt so fancy that they reached out every week, always on time; they kept showing me how much they cared about me, how much they wanted me.

At least once a month, I would receive a letter from the Clay family, something Oksana would write ME a letter, and sometimes mom used Google translate, which was funny because the translation wasn't always accurate. In each letter, Mom tried to send me a few pictures of family and sometimes small bracelets that could fit into a card. It made me feel even more special. It made me feel as if I had never left and was with them the entire time.

After I told the Proshak family that I was getting adopted, they seemed sad. But it wasn't the jealous type of sad; it was "good for you I'm going to miss you" type of sad. One weekend, the Proshak family asked me to sleepover at their place, and they wanted to meet my future family. I thought that was a really great idea, considering how much I loved both of the families and how much the Proshak family meant to me. Thanks to the Proshak family, we were able to Skype the Clay family, and I was able to see everyone; it felt so real. Anna Proshak was fluent in English, so there wasn't any misunderstanding or trouble with the communication. I sat right next to Anna, and I smiled the whole time. I mean, I probably looked stupid sitting there, smiling and waving. I had no idea what they were talking about, but I was still excited to be there and see everyone - so I just sat there with a huge smile on my face. But the conversation went on and on and on for hours. I don't think my face ever hurt like that from smiling so much.

As the fall got cooler and cooler, I developed stronger relationships with people with whom I thought I could never be friends with. For the first time ever, I had a nickname that wasn't actually offensive, like "krisa" which actually translates to rat. People called me "krisa" because it sounded the same as my name Kristina, and at times, as such, it made me hate my name. "Nadia" was my new cool nickname.

One evening, my friend Anya and I just came back from the store, so our pockets were FILLED with sunflower seeds. The boys were playing a casual soccer game, and everyone was welcome to watch. As Anya and I were making our way to the stadium, we heard "Nadia, Nadia, give me some sunflower seeds." It was Denis, who later became one of my closest friends. But at the orphanage, we hated each other; he said he called me Nadia because I looked like one but mainly because he forgot my actual name... Well you know how fast rumors spread. Within days, everyone called me "Nadia." The funny part is that we actually had one girl named Nadia; she was a year older than me. One time, Larissa Kanstantinovna called, "Nadia, come over here". Nadia and I were walking not too far away from each other, so we both turned. Nadia and I laughed, but that was the moment we became friends. I told Nadia that I had a grandmother named Nadia. Nadia wasn't even upset that she was no longer the only Nadia at the orphanage. Since Nadia was a couple of years older, she offered me my grandmother; you know, everyone had pretend parents, and I had a pretended grandmother.

Going into ninth grade, I was able to move into a bedroom with older girls or girls from my class. By this time, we had four girls in our class and this was progress. Dasha, Olga, Anya, and I were able to live together, along with a few older girls from the 10th and 11th grades. It finally felt like my life was falling into the right places, and now I was able to have a safe place where I could gossip with my girls and not have to worry about other supervisors who hated my guts.

Although, moving in together with the girls from my class didn't make us besties as I thought it would. Dasha was "too cool" to hang out with us because she was too busy having sex with her cool boyfriend Vova. One time while Dasha and her lover were doing their business, Marina Kanstantinovna walked in on them, and you can only imagine what happened next... she quickly grabbed Dasha by her hair and pushed her around a bit, of course, after calling her a whore a few times. Gave Vova a speech, and since then, we haven't seen or even heard from Dasha about her sex life. But don't get fooled; this only means that they have moved to "safer" locations where no one can disturb them. Locations like the boy's bathroom, behind the shed, or even Vova's bedroom, where he made someone way younger than him to stay alert outside of the bedroom in case a supervisor was coming.

Olga and I had somewhat of a closer relationship. In class, sometimes we sat next to each other and even listened to music together on her fancy phone in our free time. But on the weekends, Olga would go home to see a relative. When she would come back, she would tell me some wild stories that had happened to her on the weekends. Obviously, she didn't just see and stay home with her relatives. She went out and did things she couldn't do at the orphanage.

I was never allowed to see my family or go visit them on the holidays. My family lived approximately four hours away from the orphanage, and even if they did live closer, I still wouldn't be able to see them because my grandmother lost custody of me. In the beginning of my orphanage journey, I was definitely angry with the fact that my family wasn't coming to see me on the weekends or that I wasn't able to see them, but by this point in life, I just accepted the fact that my life would never be the same, that something else is waiting for me. Good or bad.

Even though we had girls in our grade, Anya and I were still the closest. Maybe because I had no one else just like her or because Olga and Dasha made fun of Anya. For the past few years, Anya has lived with her sister Masha, who is two years older than Anya, and her friends have taken care of Anya. Yet now Masha's grade graduated, and they moved on, maybe going to the local institutions in Zaporizhzhia, many moved back home, and I am not sure what happened to Masha, but what I do know is that Anya needed her. Anya was miserable without her.

THE AMERICAN CHRISTMAS

Since I came back from my first trip to America, all eyes were on me. Now, I dressed differently, I used different shower equipment, I "spoke" English, and I even smelled differently. I was making friends faster than I was failing classes. Yeah, you might say that now that I had all the fancy things, that's the only reason people have started paying attention to me, and I will say you aren't wrong. It's the orphanage. It's like War on Drugs, but here, you have to survive and try to make something out of yourself. I was making connections with all types of people, so I would say it was a win-win situation. I was friends with older girls who were flying to Italy for the summer and winter vacations and who were also bringing me gifts like I did for them. We were also making exchanges of our own. There was this girl, her name was Galya. She was a class higher, and she had a family in Italy who loved her very much, but Galya didn't want to be adopted into their family. So, this family hosted her twice a year till she graduated from the orphanage. One time, she came up to me and commented on how cool my shorts were and that she heard good things about the company. To me, they were just a pair of shorts, and I had no idea who or what this company was. So, I told Galya I would trade the pair of shorts she liked for her red pants. She hesitated at first, but our trade was successful.

I cannot tell you how many times Larissa Kanstantinovna got me into trouble with those pants. Every time she would see me wearing those pants, she would literally tell me I looked like a hooker from the streets. It got to the point where I had to hide from her but… she would still see me wearing them, and no, she wouldn't chase after me or anything; she made someone else to do so. A student would come up to me and tell me that Larissa Kanstantinovna was calling me to her office. I would of course, change the pants before I would go see her; I thought I was so slick. Yet, she knew. She always knew everything. I don't know how?! But she knew. But me being in denial about wearing those bright red pants again made me look like an idiot. She would yell at me in her office, saying something like, "Do you want me to call your American family and tell them that you are being ungrateful??? Is that what you want?! Because I can do that right quick!!! I can tell them that you aren't listening and to cancel the adoption process???" I, of course looked so guilty while staring with my head down unto my shoes. I would mumble that I was sorry and beg her not to call my American family. Larissa Kanstantinovna would NEVER sabotage anyone's adoption; she always wanted every single student to find a family who would take care of us. Of course, if it's international, it's better because Ukrainian families only want to adopt kids till they are 18 years old, so the government pays the support money. But the checks stop coming in after the student turns 18 and then they are back living on the streets. It's actually super messed up.

We had one incident where a Ukrainian family came to our orphanage to adopt a girl named Dasha, not the Dasha from my class but another Dasha. Larissa Kanstantinovna kind of warned her to be careful because she was one year away from turning 18. Dasha said that this family was different, that they were loving because they had two little girls, and they didn't seem to be that type of material who would kick her out after her 18th birthday. When the time came closer for Dasha's adoption, she told the family that she won't get adopted without her best friend Sveta; surprisingly, the family didn't seem to have an issue with adopting two 17-year-olds. When Dasha's 18th birthday came around, her fairy tale came to an end, and she and Sveta were back at the orphanage crying into a pillow on how unfair this world was. Luckily, they were able to finish the school year at the orphanage and go to a university. At this moment in life, Dasha has a beautiful daugher and her own business in Ukraine. Sveta is married and has a beautiful son.

THE AMERICAN CHRISTMAS

Just like that, December was knocking on our doors. My friends were packing their bags to visit their host families in Italy and Spain, and I, of course, was waiting for my day to do the same. This year's supervisor was Valentina Nicolaevna, which, to be honest, I was not excited about because she was not a fan of mine, and I felt the exact same way about her. But I wasn't going to ruin my trip because of her. I thought to myself that if I do everything that I was being asked to, there weren't going to be any problems. Plus, I wouldn't want Valentina Nicolaevna to snitch on whatever it is I would do to my host family, and since she and I were not besties, I had to be on my best behavior. This trip, we didn't have a lot of kids coming from my orphanage. Some kids were the same, and some were different. Lena, Sasha, and I were going to stay with our families from the summer visits Katy was going to a different host family, and this was Dima's first American visit. Surprisingly, we didn't have any issues with Valentina Nicolaevna. The train ride to the capital was just fine, of course ignoring the fact that we got our seats right next to the bathroom and the whole night it was "SLAM" "SLAM", the door sliding back and forth. On top of that, I slept on the top shelf, and the whole night I was scared that I was gonna fall off.

When we arrived at the airport, it was really nice to see some familiar faces, and it felt good to have people who were just as excited to see me. For this year's visit, we had to wear bright, bright yellow hats, which were absolutely brick out, and we had to substitute our summer shirts with a hat so we would stand out and so we wouldn't get lost. You can already guess that my friends and I were "too cool" to wear those hats, so we would hold them in our hands, and whenever a supervisor was coming, we'd put them on and take them off right after. So slick right?! When the time of getting on the plane arrived I was not scared, I knew exactly what to expect, and I brought a pack of gum and knew what to do if my ears weren't working like last time. I was ready.

Once we landed in Germany, I knew that the second flight was going to be a lot tougher because it was a lot longer. The airplane itself was huge too. Had three rows of seats, we got fed at least three times, and we just watched movies all flight. Sleeping was almost impossible on the plane. Of course, on our second flight, our supervisors passed out the letters from our families. It was one of the warmest feelings in the world. Someone out there on the other side of the globe was waiting to see me? It was really hard to believe. Once we landed in New York, I knew exactly who to look for, and with a giant smile on my face, I was scamming the crowd for Oksana. There she was… holding another poster with my ugly picture saying, "Welcome Home." There I was, hugging everyone: Oksana, Sergey, Nick and my future parents; life couldn't get any better. I felt safe. I felt loved. I was home.

The airport was decorated with lights and small decorations throughout. Every now and than there was another giant Christmas tree, bringing smiles to everyone who walked by. I asked Oksana "Take a picture" every other tree, and everyone would laugh at me. Except for Nick and Sergey; they were annoyed with me already. New York on the outside was also filled with all types of Christmas lights, and small houses outside of the hotels were shining from their outside decorations being too bright. Just like last time, we had to spend the night in New York because we had to make sure the families who were still traveling to get home in the morning were going to get on the flight safely. Which of course, I had no problem with. I am a sucker for hotels breakfasts, you could say. I felt pretty confident. I knew the family that I was staying with, where I was staying, and that I was going to make lots of great memories on this trip.

THE AMERICAN CHRISTMAS

On our drive to New Hampshire, we stopped for lunch at some fried place that had a LOT of chicken to offer, I was weirded out for sure. I've never seen such a thing, just to later find out that we were at Kentucky Fried Chicken, which didn't do a lot to me because we don't have that in Ukraine, I should say, but it might say something to you. The majority of the ride was spent with me and Oksana listening to music on her fancy pink Apple player. We were listening to some Russian banners and can't forget the early 2000s. Of course, I knew some of the songs and I had to pretend like I was fluent in English so I could sing along. In Ukraine, almost every single TV channel comes with a channel called M1; 24/7, they are constantly playing American songs from Rihanna, to name it. Even some of the radio stations played American music. So, I wasn't completely a cave man. When I got my first smartphone, and a popular song was getting announced on a radio, I would tell my grandparents to stay quiet so I could record the song and have it on my phone. You can imagine that it wasn't the best quality but that's how we used to survive back in the day. When the Bluetooth was around, we used to use it to exchange songs with one another, but when times were hard, you had what was available. At times, we asked the boys to pass some snacks around from the trunk; mom always packed something delicious for the road trips.

Pulling into the driveway was probably one of the best feelings because it felt like a vacation home, except the difference now was that this vacation home was soon enough to turn into my forever home. The best part about home was probably sharing the bedroom with Oksana, she may think otherwise, but I was and still am a sucker for the past and deep memories conversations. Oksana and I spend way too many nights staying up and whispering about our biological parents and where our lives went to shit. I liked to picture an image in my head and try to understand what Oksana's life was like back then. And even if I did understand what Oksana's life was like back in Ukraine, it didn't mean anything; I still had no idea of how she lived with the untold stories that she was too afraid to share, maybe because of fear or sadness or maybe even shame. I know I have those types of stories where I don't even know who that little girl was who lives inside my memories, it's hard to believe that it was me. It's hard to believe that's what my reality was, that that's what I thought normal was.

When we arrived at the Clay house, soon to be mine, the twin bed was waiting for my arrival in Oksana's room. On the top of the bed was a little basket of new things, all for me. I never had anyone surprise me with such things, and even though it was all the necessities like socks and shampoo I felt important and thought of - and that's the feeling that I will never forget. Because now I was the center of attention, I had all eyes on me, and not in the bad way either. This was a reunion where I felt like I was a 5th cousin who was finally reuniting with her family. Of course, the most memorable thing about this visit was Christmas and getting ready for Christmas Day. It was everything like they show us in movies; picking out a Christmas tree as a family, decorating it as a family and drinking hot coco while "Elf" is playing in the background, I mean, what else I should've dreamed of? The girls of the family had to do last-minute shopping, while the boys did everything last minute, Mom said that's what they normally do. On Christmas Eve, as a family tradition, we read Polar Express in both English and Russian, and then later that day, we watched the movie. Oksana and I helped mom wrap the gifts for the stocking, She called us her little elve's. When it was time for us to wrap each, the other person had to leave the room, which was not a problem at all because later that night I'd come to Oksana all excited and say "I'll tell you one thing from your stocking if you tell me one." To finish Christmas Eve, we all dressed real nice and went to a church to get some blessings. Which of course, I have never done before...

Before I came to America, I had no idea what stockings were?! People do celebrate Christmas in Ukraine but in different ways. Those who are Christians, celebrate Jesus's birthday at the church with Christian music, poems, and food. I should probably mention that Ukrainian Christmas is on January 6th -7th, and December 24th – 25th is just a regular day just like any other. Yet, what I grew up doing on Christmas night is after my grandmother would make the traditional food of "Christmas" called "kutya", which is made of white rice and mixed with jelly and some sugar. Traditionally, you'd bring a plate to your godmother and/or godfather, and they are supposed to give you a plate of "kutya" to bring home as well. But since my godfather, whose name is Dima, lived about 20 minutes away walking distance, I was too scared of the dark to walk that far to bring him a plate of kutya; plus, he was a drunk, so it didn't matter anyways. My relationship with my godfather was weird, you could say. He was never around when he was sober, besides that one time when he and my aunt dated?! Which I would say was really weird to me... other times, he was around to be my grandfather's drinking partner, but never to see ME.

One time, Dima came to see me on my birthday, and even though he was really drunk, he was still really excited. He was excited to give me a gift; we were poor, and our family's friends were poor, so I never expected anything from anyone. He wanted to gift me a pair of gold earrings. They were absolutely stunning, and even though, at that particular moment, I didn't have my ears pierced, it was an incredibly beautiful and thoughtful gift. Until Dima stole them from me so he could buy some alcohol.

My Godmother Natasha and my relationship is a whole different story. I think my grandfather insulted her family way too many times because they were too rich for us, and we were too poor for them. I mean, if I think correctly, I have never been inside her house, not even past her fence gate. All because my grandfather stole from them a couple of times, they didn't trust us. After they found out that I began to run away they didn't want anything to do with me, not that they were doing anything with me before. But they even stopped saying "hi." So, on Christmas night, instead of bringing kutya to my godmother and godfather, I had to bring it across the street to my grandmother's friends and our neighbors as well. Who were, at times, very nice ladies, but there were also times when those exact ladies were the first ones in line to talk shit and spread rumors.

The night before Christmas, I could not sleep... Oksana and I spoke half of the night, talking about Christmas and how we usually spend the holiday. At some point, Oksana pretty much told me to shut up and get some rest. It was really hard to force myself to fall asleep. Inside of my stomach were all types of butterflies and rollercoasters. Just as I closed my eyes, Oksana's alarm went off – the clock showed 6 A.M. Wearing my cute pjs I rushed downstairs, and our Christmas tree looked straight up out of a magazine; near the fire pit were our stockings with our names that were absolutely overflowing with gifts. You can imagine that it took a hot minute to make our parents get up, and of course, they must have at least one cup of coffee before we can start opening the gifts. But even then, every moment of that day was magical. Opening the gifts, I probably looked like a six-year-old girl who still believes that Santa is real. We spent the rest of the afternoon hanging out in our pjs, eating some delicious food, and watching Christmas movies. Christmas at the Clay's was a success.

THE AMERICAN CHRISTMAS

Even though the winter visit is a bit shorter than the summer visit, that didn't stop Mom from planning the cool things for us to do. We spend the rest of my visit going tubing, pottery, and some shopping, of course. For the last week of my visit, Valentina Nicolaevna stayed with us... which a part of me was not a fan, of course but the second half of me was excited to show her all of my cool things I got for Christmas. I was excited that she could spend some quality time not only with me but with my future family as well, to get to know the family that I was staying with and would be living with soon. To be honest, I didn't really know Valentinu Nicolaevnu outside of work. As she stayed with us, I think it gave me a chance to really get to know her and I guess, what makes her who she is. We got a chance to truly bond with each other. We cooked and baked together, and Mom took us shopping. We got a chance to do things that we were not able to at the orphanage, and just like that, Valentina Nicolaevna became my friend. Later, we shared some memories and even inside jokes that no one got. Made me feel pretty cool.

Of course, every vacation and visit at some point has to come to an end, and even though I didn't want to leave America and leave my future family and of course, my new bff Oksana, I was excited to come back to my motherland, Ukraine. The whole family drove us to New York, where we ended up spending the night because most of the kids had either longer flights because they lived farther away. It was definitely a very warm feeling to be surrounded by so many kids who were speaking the same language at the same place. Gave me a feeling of home, and seeing my friends made me miss the people who weren't with us. I kept getting increasingly excited about going home because I knew I had people waiting for me on the other side of the world. Saying goodbye always is the hardest part; not knowing what will happen to me in Ukraine and what will happen to my future family, being apart and living so far away from each other was tough. Every decision that I made or was about to make, I had to think about because I didn't want my future family to change their mind and get rid of me. Because deep down, I knew they could I knew that they had the power to say yes or no if needed. And from personal experience, I knew that I was the problem child with issues or whatever and people are okay with living or walking out because, at the end of the day, there is always someone smarter, prettier, and just better. I mean I looked like a sad boy when Kevin just saw me for the first time, yet he still wanted me as his daughter.

Larissa Kanstantinovna made us celebrate every holiday on the calendar that ever existed. Sometimes, a part of me felt like, "why are we doing this? It's a waste of time," yet sometimes it felt needed. Living at the orphanage with the exact same schedule every single day could get pretty depressing and boring. You wake up, and you already know what the next month will look like with no changes. I think her goal was to make us feel something. To remind us that holidays are about being together, to feel joy of celebrating and of course to have fun. For every holiday, every grade had to come up with something to present at the concert or the show that we would have for whatever holiday we were celebrating. We didn't have that much space or a stage or a theater, so we would have our shows in a cafeteria. After pushing out the chairs and tables, we would roll out this long, beautiful rug; the walls would always have some kind of hangings to make them look festive. Some kids would sing, some kids would dance, and tell poems, but I wasn't good at anything, so I was just a part of the audience as always. There were few moments when I was a backup dancer, and me and a few other girls even went to a concert to represent our orphanage. I think we scored third place. However, overall, I was a brick when it came to dancing.

It always took me the longest to remember the moves, and I had a hard time staying on beat. Others were good at boxing, soccer, drawing, and even gymnastics, yet I was that kid you'd find sitting in the back on the bleachers. The sad part about this… is that Larissa Kanstantinovna would reward every single participant with a huge chocolate bar. Of course, I had many friends who participated in many events, and they would share. However, it's not the same as being the one who gets it; it's just another moment of feeling unworthy enough.

CHAPTER 8

THIRD TIME IS A CHARM

May. The school is out. Finals are passed. Hearing the sound of the bells. Standing in a single line. Boys and girls wearing white tops and black bottoms all around except us. All eyes on us. We are the center of all attention, and oh well, it is deserved. The difference between us and the rest of the students attending the celebration is that our class is wearing a yellow sash stating, "9th grade graduation year of 2014." A celebration where a bunch of 14 and 15-year-olds are getting ready to leave Larissa's Kanstantinovnas nest and fly into the world.

Photo #1 the graduation class of 2014 making the big walk-in front of the whole orphanage, surrounded by family members, classmates, and peers. Taking the lead by the class teacher Irina Vladimirovna holding hand with a former student Gena (it's a tradition people stay calm)

Photo #2 a graduation picture with almost the whole class. (Ya, so you can see why I was freaked out by American high school).

About 90% of my classmates asked Larissa Kanstantinovna if they could leave the orphanage after graduating the 9th grade. And believe it or not most of them left. I think that the reason why Larissa Kanstantinovna has to approve their leave is that you have to have a good reason. The majority of the students went to a university. Of course, the university wasn't anything crazy. I mean, some dorms had broken windows while it was snowing outside and the university was in no rush to fix, soooo you get the idea. And two students left because they had jobs they wanted to attend. I didn't even ask. I had nothing outside the orphanage walls waiting for me besides going home to the village. Because my 10th grade class was so small (four students), they combined the 10th and 11th grades further down the road after I left the orphanage.

I remember throwing the biggest tantrum about the fact that, as a 10th grader, we were forced to learn German and not English. I was told that the English language is for the upper class, like the 11th grade. I told everyone that I don't need the orphanage half-effort education because I won't be here any longer. When I just found out that in 10th grade, students learn German language, I wanted to cry. Not because the German language isn't hard and complicated, because it is, and not because I was not smart enough because I wasn't. But because of the conflict between Germany and Ukraine that happened ages ago… Besides, is Germany teaching Ukrainian to their people? Because I don't believe so. Our German teacher was the tiniest and the most fraudal person ever… and I did not give her the respect she deserved. Our whole grade did not listen to her, and we had zero passion to actually learn the language… I've definitely made her cry by screaming in her face and saying that her lesson plans were a waste of my time and hers because I needed to learn English. Sometimes, she would run out of the classroom crying and screaming, "monsters."

Of course, now I feel really bad, and we have talked a few times since I got adopted. She still teaches at the orphanage, and I just don't know how she did it all, but she still does. She is one of many teachers who deserve a medal.

I also knew that I had the flexibility to get into trouble and just act as wild as I pleased because there was no way that Larissa Kanstantinovna would have made me stay in Ukraine and not let me get adopted, and I don't want to say that I abused the situation, but maybe that's how it was. Maybe I knew that I was unstoppable? Or maybe this was me showing my true colors because I was finally comfortable with being who I was and the kind of people I was surrounded with. As bad as it sounds but I think that this is when I was finally happy with who I was, and I finally accepted because I knew that someone out there in the middle of nowhere and across the freaking ocean, someone who wanted me. They wanted me for who I was with all the ugly and pretty.

Around May, everyone was trying to figure out where and with whom they will spend their summer. I was told that many directors from different orphanages could not afford to keep between 200-300 kids just walking around and getting into trouble at the orphanage. One – because they couldn't afford to feed us and two – because who would stay to supervise us? Because the teachers and the cook, and the janitor also need and deserve a break from all of the crap that I and everyone else have put those people through.

So, I think sometime before the summer starts, all of the directors from different regions meet and they discuss how much they have and what every orphanage can afford and at the end of the meeting, they find a happy medium and they pick out a summer camp that works for everyone. When the name of the summer camp was announced, everyone reached out to their friends from different orphanages to see what summer camp they were going to.

Now, there were times when not every orphanage agreed on one camp because of the budget provided for them. So, there were times when there were three camps built right next to each other, and you could see what kind of orphanage was there. You could tell if they were poor or rich or if they had sponsors. I mean, if the summer camp is buji and they have bananas and smoothies for breakfast, who could afford them? Of course, there were times when me and my friends were made fun of because, one – we were sent there as a whole orphanage or two – because the type of camp we stayed at was sometimes not that great, especially when you have something fancier right next to you so people can see the difference. Also, if the camp is Buji, it wasn't common for parents to send their kids to the same camp as the orphanage kids. Well, packing my suitcase for the summer camp was not my priority yet… my priority was to get my visa open and bring the biggest suitcase there is with absolutely nothing. You think I'm joking huh? But that was the mode of our orphanage, you know why? "Because your new family can buy you new everything."

Every new hosting season, there were less and less kids who were coming from our orphanage because no new kids were coming in, and I guess the families needed "fresh meat" that we didn't have... welp... this hosting season, we did get a piece of new meat. Not necessarily "new" to the orphanage, but he for sure was new to this hosting thing. His name was Denis and he's been at the orphanage for a long time, I would say, and of course, he was one of the troubled kids because of the crowd that he was hanging out with who were, of course a bunch of idiots. Denis was a grade below me, and his grade literally didn't have a single girl for a long time. When a girl started attending the classes in his grade, she was an outsider. Mostly because she wasn't an orphan, and her parents sent her to attend classes at the orphanage because it's cheaper than normal education. Of course, she was now the only girl in her whole class: one girl and 15 guys.

Well, even though Denis' grade was on the soccer team, and they were bringing medals from boxing competitions, they were still idiots because after a long game of scoring of whatever, they would reward themselves by smelling shoe glue out of a plastic bag so they could get high. I couldn't stand Denis!!! He was cocky and always needy, and he thought that just because he was spending time together with the soccer boys, he was mister popular. Even though Denis and I physically fought when I just arrived at the orphanage, and even though Denis was one of the shortest guys in his grade and he was still able to bully me When I found out that Denis was coming to America with me and how dare him being on the same plane as me, well, anyways I was pissed... than I told myself that it would only be for a good 48 hours and besides I wouldn't have to stand next to him the whole time?! I also reminded myself that hopefully, there would be plenty of other people from different orphanages that were officially my besties. Therefore, I could just ignore Denis the whole time. Besides, why would I even think that he would want to spend some time with me or be near me or even talk to me?! Like I said, we hated each other very much.

Of course, by this time, I was a professional. I knew where we were going, I knew what kind of people in different buildings were, and I knew around what type of people to watch my mouth and watch my language... I knew where the train station was and where to track our trains, I knew where the airport was, and I knew which way to go. I was proudly walking next to the supervisors and leading the pack with my head high. This year's supervisor was named Natasha. She was really friendly, even though I didn't know much about her because she was mainly one of Denis' teachers and taught lower classmates. Funny, but even though she seemed like she could defend herself, she was very fragile on the outside, but she always knew how to put all those boys in their places, and they even respected her, which was very uncommon at my orphanage So she must be doing something right?! Anyways, there were about three boys from Denis's grade who were coming on this trip.

One of the boys didn't know that he was going into this other guy's hosting family until we all got our letters from our hosting families. Believe it or not, but those two boys didn't like each other. One was from 8th grade, and the other one was from 7th grade, and of course, the older guy bullied the younger guy for many reasons too. When all of us found out that the two are staying in the same family, we all were in shock really. And I'm sure the boys felt the same way as well. Denis didn't really have a family that he was going to stay for the whole visit; however, he was going to bounce between families in hopes of finding a forever family that could remind him of what parental love really feels like. I knew that Denis wasn't really an orphan because he still had a family of some sort. He had his sister, and I believe she is married and has a daughter, which makes Denis an uncle, which is surprising to all of us I know. But believe it or not, he loves his niece, and I am sure that he would do anything for her. I know that he also had a Grandmother that took care of him, and sometimes on the weekends, he would visit her and his sister. I know that I'm making Denis sound like he is a monster. I'm sure his family loved him for who he was and whatever the trouble he got into, but he was a monster in my eyes who bullied me; who would punch a girl for a piece of candy or the last piece of bread if it ever came to it.

When we arrived at the airport in New York, I knew exactly who to look for yet again; like I said, I was a pro by now and knew everything. My eyes were searching for Oksana, out of all the people in this place, this family, and overall, the country. She was my person. When my eyes met hers, we rushed into each other's arms with giant smiles on our faces. This is what love felt like. This is what home is supposed to feel like: being wanted. I knew that we weren't going to New Hampshire just yet. I knew the drill; we had to make sure that other children landed safely in other states and that the families were okay with traveling home as well.

For some reason, Denis wasn't leaving and at first, I was wondering if his host family hadn't arrived or if they were late. Yet, when I asked Oksana, she told me that Denis was going to stay with another supervisor from the Open Heart and Homes organization, which was not too far in Philadelphia. So, the supervisor of the program just like my parents, had to wait around to make sure there were no issues with any other children. I thought to myself that if I had to spend another day with this kid, I don't know what I would do because now it was harder to hide away from or to ignore him because, with time, other kids were leaving to go to their states with their families and here we were.

Eating breakfast at the table for eight, where everything was awkward, like making eye contact every five minutes. Not on purpose of course. Even though we were surrounded by a small group of people, Denis still found a way to either make fun of me or to, make sure I would trip over his foot, or even flip me off and call me names. Of course, the adults had no idea what he was saying to me, and I didn't want to be a snitch, so I didn't say anything to them. However, I would cry to Oksana about how I wanted to be home, be far away from this immature child.

It wasn't too late after Denis and his host Dad hit the road and were on their way home, and so were we. Of course, once we got home, a twin-size bed was waiting for me in Oksana's bedroom. On top of the bed was a small package waiting for me, and as always, Mom knew how to deliver a surprise. Inside the package, there were some socks, underwear, candy, some things to color, and a stuffed animal, which later became my cuddle buddy at nighttime. Within a few weeks, Mom and Oksana of course, took me shopping for new clothes, and it was super fun because no one had bought me new clothes in what felt like ages. Yeah, at the orphanage, they would give out "new" clothes, but they didn't ask us what size we were or if we liked what was provided. We just had to wear what we had because we didn't have anything else. The outside people called us "incubators" because we all dressed alike.

Once I finally settled in with the time change and American food I was thriving for sure. Going to the pool almost every day, annoying my older future brothers as I should. Oksana even tried teaching me how to play big tennis, but my arms were not strong enough more like noodle arms. Once July came around, we as the whole family, went to a parade in the center of our town for the 4th of July celebration. Where people who were walking in the parade were throwing out food at kids?? Sign me up! The parade itself wasn't that long, and I got to walk away from pockets filled with American candy, which I'm a little surprised how my teeth didn't fall out that day. But after the parade, we walked around to see what kind of goodies people from nearby brought to either sell or to give away. Some people even brought dogs and goats for people to pet. I was the first one in line to pet any sort of animal and take a picture with them, of course.

As the summer continued, I was told that we will be going to Canabie Lake Park, which is located near by us and isn't too far of a drive, maybe like an hour away. We were all going as a family to ride all sorts of rides, and I have never been to this one before, so I was excited to explore. However, I was also told that we were going to meet up with Denis and after the park he was coming to stay with us… for the rest of the trip. FOR THE REST OF THE TRIP???? I most definitely had a "are you kidding me" face on. But! I was in no position to say anything against that because, technically, I was just a visitor myself?! Mom told me that the supervisor, Natasha would be staying with us for the rest of the trip as well. I knew I had to keep my cool and just ignore him. He should be the one who should be nervous and scared because he was coming to stay with my future family in my future house! The park was awesome, and it seemed like my older brother Sergey was hitting it off with Denis, yet of course, I was jealous that my future brother was having more fun with him and not me… But I had to remember that they are boys or whatever. So, I just stuck with my bestie Oksana, and we were on a whole different level; we don't need no boys to have fun.

The first few days, like I said, I was ignoring him, and I was doing my own thing, but Mom over here needed to include Denis in everything that used to be mine and Oksana's. Oksana and I used to go to the pool together, but now Denis comes with us. Oh, Oksana wants to go play big tennis and Tina isn't strong enough to hold the racket; guess who is, though? Denis. I was heated like a bull, and I wanted to go home so badly just so I would get away from his face because now he was everywhere!! He was at the dinner table eating the watermelon that I picked out and cut. He was cutting me off in line to take a shower. He was picking out a movie for everyone to watch. He was bonding with the boys, and he was stealing Oksana from me.

In the photo: Natalia & Tetiana, my sister Oksana and I –wearing matching pajamas.

I was beyond excited to have someone I knew in my future home with me, and I was excited to get to know her outside of work, which is almost impossible at the orphanage. Yet, when Natasha arrived, I still felt like an outsider because Denis was her boy, and I was just a girl she knew from the orphanage. I was not mad at her for bonding with Denis over me. I was also not mad at her for bonding with Oksana because she was older and more mature than me. Of course, as the days went on, we began to develop a relationship where we would cook meals together, and she would provide medication every time my nose was runny. And maybe those were her duties and responsibilities as a chaperone, but who knows? I felt like the friendship was there.

In this photo: Denis, our supervisor Natalia and i at the pool

Towards the end of our stay in America, it was surprising that Denis and I became best friends after our stay there. This summer brought us together, and we have gotten to know each other on deeper levels – the pretty and the ugly. We shared our stories and how we got ourselves to what felt like the bottom of a pyramid and let people wipe their feet all over us at the orphanage. We spent the nights talking about what we would do once we got back to Ukraine, who we were excited to see at the orphanage, and what summer camp we were going to. Because we knew well that this would be my last summer camp, I would strongly say that at the end of this American summer, Denis and I were friends.

Of course, my family's plan was to find a loving family for Denis. The organization was doing everything they could to find his forever home. One evening, we all went to a Slavic Church about 30 minutes away from our house. I loved going there for obvious reasons - because being surrounded by this community felt like home. It reminded me how nice it will be to get back to my homeland, be around my native language, and feel i belong. Mom and Dad tried their best to bring us there because they always had food (one of my favorite reasons of course), but also because they knew how important the holidays were to us. For example, in America, people don't celebrate New Year as much as they do in Ukraine. In Ukraine, New Year is one of the biggest holidays, and people party non-stop for days. People also believe that in order to have a successful year, you must end it successfully. My grandmother used to make sure that we had 12 different dishes on our table to have a good start to a new year. Each meal would represent a month. Maybe that's why New Year was one of my favorite holidays, because of all the food that I got to eat.

At the Slavic Church Mom made a slide show where she talked to people about who she was and why families should consider adopting Denis. Of course, Oksana and I were there to help encourage the families by sharing a real-life situation and scenarios based on our stories. And of course, Denis was there, and he spoke for himself and told the audience why he wanted a family and why coming to America would save his life from becoming something he wasn't or was afraid of becoming because of his family background. You know how it is... show me your friends, and I will tell you who you are. Well, in this case, show me your family, and I will assume your future. Which is unfair if you'd ask me because half of the time, kids don't end up being like their parents or their family, yet most of the time, they do because everyone around has already given up on them. They have absolutely no support around them, so yes, they have no other choice but to end up being like their family.

After leaving the Slavic Church, I'm not even sure if Denis had any hopes about his future or finding a family who would take him, but what I was sure about was the fact that Denis and I had become the closest friends. As our American summer was ending, we had spent every evening imagining what we would do in the summer camp or once we would get back to the orphanage. First of all, we knew that everyone around us would be shocked to see that we weren't trying to rip each other's hair anymore, or the fact that we stopped calling each other names. Or even the fact that we considered each other friends. Crazy what one summer can do.

Saying goodbye to my future family has always been hard, but I knew that I would come back and see them again. I knew that next Winter or summer hosting season, I would be on the list, and I would travel miles and miles across the ocean to see them. Yet, this time was different. This time, I was not coming back for any hosting visits. I was not coming back to America as an orphan; this time, I would come back as an American citizen who had a family. A whole family to be exact, is the type of family that has a father, a mother and six other siblings. I was freaking out. At this point, I had absolutely no time to process what was going on because everything was happening so damn fast. And if I had a time machine, I would have paused the time just for a slight moment. I was not as sad this time about leaving. All I knew is that the little time I had to spend as a

Ukrainian citizen in my homeland was limited, and I had to live it to the fullest. Of course, I spent the nights talking to Oksana about the things that I wanted to do once I came to America, things like dying my hair black or getting a tattoo. She, of course, said that if I genuinely want to do those things, I must get all that done in Ukraine because there was no way that Kevin and Aileen would let me do so. I smirked back at her and knew exactly what I had to do.

Leaving my future family sight was hard and sad. But that sadness was temporary because the second I saw my friends or familiar faces, I knew we were a few steps closer to being home. At the hotel, the night before everyone would arrive, all of the kids would divide into groups based on what orphanage they came from. This makes perfect sense because why would I want to share my summer visit with kids I barely know? That's silly... but of course, we would talk to other kids our age, with whom through so many visits, we would develop strong bonds and relationships.

Traveling back wasn't as scary; we knew what to expect. Before leaving the country, Oksana gave me about 200 grins that she had saved from her travels. She wanted to save the money to remember how they looked, but in America, Ukrainian money had no value. She told me to make good use of it. Also, every American family gives a chaperone about $20 for a meal per child. But we were too smart for that; we would save the money and not spend it on meals, or we would eat at Puzata Hata, which literally translates to "Fat House." Puzata Hata is a chain restaurant that serves more buffet-style food and only serves traditional Ukrainian food. Who wouldn't want a cup of fresh borscht or have a taste of a Kievskoi katleti? But what doesn't get spent on the meal we would get the change, which would be around 150-100 grivnas. Once we arrived at the Kievskiy vokzal, we knew exactly what to do, so we all stuck to the same plan, saying that we were not hungry. Once we landed, I knew I had to call my aunt to let her know that I was okay and everything was okay. Believe it or not, she told me she was in Kyiv visiting her father, aka my grandfather, because he had gotten a new job as a taxi driver all the way in the capital. She offered to come to see me because it has been a while since I've seen her pretty face or talked to her in person. She told me that things back at home were not going so well. My grandfather needed a job, and he got one. However, his buddies at work kept bullying him and stealing his money, so he has not made much of a difference since he arrived.. Even though we saw each other for a good 15 minutes, she had won over me, and I was in tears because, for a slight second, I felt bad. I blamed myself for the fact that things weren't working out for my grandfather, even though I knew he was a grown-ass man who was pretty capable of taking care of things and problems. But me being the person who I am, I took out 100 grivnas and gave it to her. She was very thankful and couldn't stop kissing me all over my face, saying how much she missed me. Within seconds, she had disappeared into the crowd of strangers. I was left standing by myself on the steps of a train station, questioning if I just supported the addiction or a loved one.

The train ride was absolutely terrible. I'm not sure if our tickets were bought at the last minute or not or if sleeping next to the bathroom is cheaper than the rest of the tickets. All I know is that it was not fun, and I would not call it sleeping. But personally, my ride was somewhat fun. On the top bunker, just on the other side of me was a boy my age. We spent most of the night talking, and I spilled all the beans about who I was, where I come from, and all my dirty secrets. I would say we were bonding until I said that I liked his necklace, and after that, I told him that I was from an orphanage and all the orphanage does is steal, so the second he would close his eyes, his necklace will be in my hands. When I tell you this boy was terrified, that's an understatement. I mean, he tried his hardest not to laugh, but me having a straight face did not help the situation, and at some point, he asked me, "why would say that?" I was able to sense his fear miles away. I couldn't help but laugh; he probably thought I was a psychopath. Anyways, long story short... when I woke up, this boy had all his belongings in his backpack underneath his pillow and was holding onto it for dear life. I couldn't help myself and giggle again.

Of course, in the morning, I told my friends and everyone from our group what had happened, and they thought it would be super funny to play tricks on him and to scare him again. I think we had traumatized this innocent human being, and I truly wonder if he had any nightmares afterwards.

Once we arrived in Zaporizhzhia, we had a fancy... just kidding, far from fancy bus waiting for us. We all had about three to four suitcases or bags or some sort of luggage. It was ridiculous if you asked me who I was to say something because I was one of those weirdos carrying a lot of stuff. The drive from the train station to the city was not bad at all, but at that point, we were all exhausted and just needed a break from traveling and a nice shower with no line. Once we arrived at the orphanage, it was all nice and quiet almost peaceful; at the steps of the entrance, there she was our favorite director, Larissa Kanstantinovna. Maybe a part of me is being sarcastic maybe not I will leave that part for you to decide. She welcomed us with hugs and kisses, but her warm side was not open to us for long. Within seconds, she was yelling with her hands in the air, saying that the bus was ready to go to bring us to the summer camp and that we only have about 20 minutes to get ready and pack; otherwise, the bus would leave without us.

CHAPTER 9
GOODBYES

The name of the summer camp was called "arlenok," which is a bird. In English, it translates to stork, baby stork to be exact. The bird that is known for either stealing babies or bringing them to families. Of course, the summer camp was on the Black Sea. If I remember it correctly, the camp was located about four-ish hours away from our orphanage. The drive time flew by really quickly, and it almost felt like as soon I blinked, we had arrived. Of course, I had to bring all the gifts that Aileen had bought for half of my grade and my friends. It wasn't anything fancy; it was mostly T-shirts, but hey, it's the thought that counts. Once we arrived, everyone rushed towards us since we all looked fancy, pulling up, wearing new drips, and rolling our fancy suitcases. Everyone who ran towards us was either asking who we were and what group we were in or asking if we brought them anything.

The groups were based on the orphanage from which we were from. The camp counselors wanted to keep it simple for us and for them as well, so they kept every orphanage together. Which at the moment, it seemed boring, since in the past, before the orphanage life, the camp counselor would separate us by age. Each group gets a whole different cabin with a bunch of bedrooms for boys and girls, one bathroom for girls and a separate bathroom for boys, and a huge hall that we would call a living room. Oh yeah, the showers were outside, where both boys and girls would shower together.

Once we were shown our orphanage cabin, I tried to look for my room. To be honest, I didn't really care where I lived because all I wanted was to see my friends, make more friends and have the rest of the summer just as good as the beginning was. Once we all got settled in, I was landed with younger girls; of course, I was mad because I didn't want to live with 5th graders. I was too cool for that. I began walking around different girl bedrooms to see who was living where with hopes that someone just as cool as me had an empty bed I could take. Luckily, it was my day. I found a bedroom where Nadia and Masha lived; they were both upper graders, two grades above me. I had a pretty close relationship with Nadia, but Masha, on the other hand… When I saw Masha on my first day at the orphanage, I made it pretty clear to myself that I would stay away from her. She was for sure, intimidating… When I walked into their room, there was a moment of silence… I didn't know what to say after I already said "Hi." It was awkward for sure. After a moment of silence, they asked me conversation-starting questions like, "How was America?" I got too excited talking about the most amazing trip of my life. I just sat down and wouldn't shut up. They were laughing at me. After a good talk, they told me I should move in. As I unpacked my suitcase, Masha saw my cool Mickie Mouse t-shirt that my friend Katya had given me because it was too big on her. It felt awkward for sure, giving her the t-shirt because it was gifted to me, but if a t-shirt is what helped our friendship to start, who cares? This day, that exact moment, was how our friendship was born. Masha pretty much took me in, and we did everything together. The first few days it was, of course, a little awkward because I was hanging out with younger girls who were also afraid of Masha, and Masha was hanging out with girls who were from her grade who were absolutely disgusted with me because they remembered me for who I was a year ago when I looked like a boy.

On my very first night at the summer camp, Yulia, Yana, Masha, and I got absolutely wasted. How exactly did we get ourselves into such a position, you may ask… on the summer camp, where each group has about two chaperones? Well… our chaperones were also there for a good time; they were two young women who were in their early twenties who spent majority of their time at their boyfriend's cabin. So it was rare that we would see them, and the times that we did see them were the times that they would ask for small favors like if we had a lighter or if we could stay in our cabins until the director did the nightly check in so they wouldn't get into trouble. And not going to lie; we did them favors and they returned them by covering for us when needed. So, when Masha said that we should celebrate our summer visit in America and the beginning of a lit summer, we all said, "say less." We all chipped in and just like that, we bought two liters of beer at some crackhead's house.

Before we knew it, we were falling all over each other and telling each other how much we loved each other. Of course, the best part about the summer camp is the "diskotekas", where we all get to dance and get away with small troubles, like sneaking in other teenagers who aren't supposed to be there. There was a moment when Yulia, Yana and I were dancing until Yulia started screaming, saying they were here. I was confused and had no idea what was happening, so I kept asking, "who's here?" They grabbed my hand and dragged me to meet a pretty large group of teenagers our age who I was told lived in the town and got invited to come to diskotekas every evening. I was told the girls met them on the beach because the beach is a public access, and everyone is allowed. And it's not like anyone cares enough to forbid us and tell us who we should spend time together with. If anything, these people came from rich families and wore nice watches, jewelry, and nice clothes. If anything, they shouldn't be hanging out with us, but here we were. Making the best memories ever.

It didn't take me long to fit in and join their friend group, and just like that, Masha, Yulia and I were sneaking out of our cabins after the whole camp goes to bed; we had to stick around for the evening check-in, where the director and another supervisor walk around each cabin and check in every bedroom to make sure that every child is in their beds. Because if you think about it, the director was responsible for all of us… yet, after the check-in, the three of us would escape through the window – all of the cabins were just a single floor. Once we were outside, we also had to make sure that no one else would see us like night watchers who walk around the camp and stay alert just in case someone else passes or escapes. However, you can also develop friendships… aka build alliances. So, once in a while, we would bring a pack of cigarettes to the security guard in return for our freedom, which worked perfectly. There were also times when the security guard fell asleep at his station.

Once the three of us would successfully get to the other side of the fence, we would meet up with our friends from the town and do all the fun things together as the whole town was asleep – well almost. One time, we met up with our friends and went night swimming; the water was so warm and calm. There were times when one of the town boys would "borrow" their father's car and all of us would make it work and fit in. There were two people sitting in the driver's seat, about two people in the passenger seat, about seven in the back seat, about five in the trunk and the rest on the roof. People were also sitting on the windows as they were down. One of the times when the car was packed, we drove into a cornfield and played hide and seek. Wild. I know. This is not something that could easily slide here in America. But it's the days like this that make me smile today.

Yeah, I mean, it was probably stupid and maybe not the smartest decision I have ever made but… some other nights we would just lay in the middle of the road and watch the stars. Some nights we would go to someone's house and just hang out at their house until the sunrise. Sneaking back into our cabin was a lot easier than sneaking out because if someone questioned us, we always had a good excuse to escape the punishment. Yet, most of the time, everyone was still sleeping or did not care enough to ask questions. Of course, by the time we'd get back to our cabins, it was almost wake-up time, yet our camp counselors did not care enough to force us to get up. I think we'd go to breakfast all together, but when everyone gets ready to go to the beach, we would nap until lunchtime. Again, no one questioned us.

One night, the three of us made plans with our town friends to meet at the bus station in front of the camp. Right at the entrance of the camp, there was a little bar that was open 24/7 so you can imagine that there were constant fights and chaos right outside of our summer camp, but again, that is no unique news and just stuff that happens on the daily basis. We made plans to meet up at 11 P.M, so for some reason, not a single friend of ours was answering their phones, we just patiently waited at the bus station. Shortly, two tipsy guys who looked like they were in their twenties approached the bus station and sat on the bench. We did not try to engage with them, but at some point, we started to giggle because they kept saying that they were waiting for a bus so they could get home. We thought it was super funny because it was past the bus time. After we got to know each other, they offered us some beer, which we politely declined, well Masha was the one who accepted it, me and Yulia did not feel as comfortable. We did not feel like we were in danger, and as minutes went by, we all were laughing our asses off. Just like that, as we were all chilling at the bus station, we heard loud noises coming from afar. A bunch of teenage boys drove by us on their mopeds with bats in their hands. When we looked closer, we recognized a few of those boys; they were our friends who never got back to us. We just stood there confused, with absolutely no right words to express what we had just seen. Masha was the first one who spoke; she was annoyed and angry, we all were. The tipsy boys tried to break the awkward moment by offering us a cigarette, and we all accepted. After smoking the whole cigarette, Masha asked for another one, and it was obvious that her emotions were up and down. The boys exchanged looks and laughed at one another.

"Wait, did I say those were cigarettes?" One of the boys said as he was still laughing. We all froze because we were afraid of the answer or what they were about to say next.

"Well, if we didn't smoke cigarettes… what the heck was that??" my heart was pounding.

"Weed," both answered again with laughter. Now, Masha was getting angrier and angrier. I mean, don't get me wrong, I was absolutely terrified of drugs, especially knowing that my Dad overdosed on them. I wanted to keep my distance from them and knowing that someone just forced them into my body, I was in shock. Angry. But if you'd look at Masha and me when we were angry, you would want to stay away from her and not me. I mean I was a twig, and she looked like she could fuck someone up. I mean, she had smoke coming out of her nostrils. She walked closely to one of the boys and said, "You better pray that I will never see you again because then you'll be in big trouble." We speed-walked away from them, and I think out of the three of us, Yulia was panicking the most.

At this point, our goal was just to get back to our cabin and just go to bed. I don't think neither of us knew how to react or what exactly we were supposed to do so we just went to bed and forced ourselves to fall asleep. As the next morning came, the three of us agreed to keep what had happened the night before on the low because the least we needed was more problems. Of course, it was already too late for that because Dasha, a girl from my grade, was already all over our business asking a lot of questions "who?" "Where?" and "how many." I mean I was not that close with her, but I knew Masha was some sort of friend with her because Dasha dated Vova, who was Masha's classmate. So, we didn't have an issue with sharing what happened. Who knew that Dasha had a big mouth? She told the story to her boyfriend, who had anger issues, just like that, the guys from our orphanage were gathering everyone around to find those guys and beat them up because they drugged us. I guess I missed the part where we were all one big family?

At this point, we had about 30 guys in our faces asking if we remembered those guys or what they looked like or where they were from. We had no idea. Truthfully, we didn't? But I guess the boys figured out that we spent time together with the town boys, so they just assumed that those are the guys who drugged us. So, they all decided to get to them at the evening diskoteka. Of course, we had to warn them because a) they were our friends and b) they weren't the ones who were responsible. But not a single of them was still answering. All we had to do was wait.

As the diskoteka began, Masha, Yulia and I couldn't just sit around or enjoy ourselves because we were freaking out. We didn't want anything to go wrong, we didn't want the boys to actually get into the fight, and lastly, we didn't want to get kicked out of the camp because that was a possibility. Once the boys arrived, we approached them and told them what they missed on out the night before and what could happen at any minute. Our goal was to try to make them leave. Yet, it was already too late for that, a little bird had already spread the word that the town boys had arrived. At this point, we only had one option to do. Yulia went up to the dj and told him to pass the message to the director that some people are trespassing and didn't belong to this camp. She immediately stopped the music and began searching for those who didn't belong there by saying a statement first.

"I received information that we have someone on this campus who broke the rules and broke in. I am going to ask you all a question; please answer honestly. If you belong here and came from an orphanage, please sit down, and those who are from this town, please remain standing and leave immediately." Of course, all of us were scared and we didn't want to get our friends or get ourselves into trouble so we told them to squat down with us, they had no idea what was happening and this clearly kept irritating the director so after few more of the up and down exercises she made a final announcement that the diskoteka was over and told everyone to go to their cabins. To not make it obvious, we had to grab them to our dorm, but we had to do it fast because we also knew who would be walking towards the same direction as our boys, and if they saw each other, it wouldn't be good.

So, we did our best by distracting everyone and bringing the town boys to the camp entrance where we thought they would be safe, where all of us would be safe. Yet, that wasn't the case whatsoever. Our boys were already there... waiting. Within seconds, we found ourselves in the crowd full of screaming, yelling, pushing, and so much more. We tried our best by separating the two parties from one another, but we failed because those boys were hungry for a fight, so we had to separate ourselves in order to stay in one piece. We did not want to engage in the fight; besides, that would mean we had to choose whose side to defend, which was not an option because all of them were our friends. Most of them from the orphanage bullied me, but I thought it was sweet that they tried to defend us. So, we just left.

GOODBYES

The next day, the boys from the orphanage were talking about how we owed them a favor because they stood up for us and defended us. Lol, but when we told them that those were not the right guys, they felt bad, which was surprising. Then, they yelled at us, saying that it was our fault that we didn't tell them to stop. Which is not true we did? They just didn't want to listen to us.

During the last couple of weeks at the summer camp, I had been crying on Masha's shoulder. Because I knew that I just had the best summer ever and the best friendships ever with a lot of cool people, and just like that, I would have to leave everything and everyone as if it never happened. All I would have were memories and it didn't seem fair. I hated the fact that so much good was happening around me. People from my orphanage began to see me as who I was and not as a girl with a boy haircut, or the girl who had holes in her socks or the girl who used the orphanage shampoo because apparently, only poor orphans did so, and I didn't have the resources to do something about it. But of course, after a year of battle I had won, and people began to care about my opinion and what I had to say in general. I finally felt like I had belonged somewhere. It finally felt like I had found my crew, my group of friends. It made me sad to know that just in two months, I had to leave everything behind me forever. I began to feel guilty because now it felt like my heart was in my homeland and not miles on miles away in some strange county.

Of course, getting on that school bus and waving goodbye to our town friends and knowing that I 100% will never see them again, laugh with them or scream from the top of my lungs into darkness in the middle of the night without knowing what time it was because no one cared. Because we all were in the moment. This was the first hard goodbye. I mean yeah, we exchanged the phone numbers and added each other on VK, but its different from being present or sitting next to each other. I had no idea that this was just the beginning of goodbyes, painful goodbyes that brought out the ugly side of me because it made me question my decision. I mean, I didn't even think about it. I haven't had the talk with my biological family; I was absolutely terrified to know what they would say if they knew.

Before school began, my aunt, my grandparents, and my mother came to visit me at the orphanage. They hired a taxi driver and drove to see me four hours away. I mean, I was impressed, don't get me wrong. It was just that too much was happening at the same time. Maybe they had a feeling that this would be the very last time they could see me, hug me, kiss me. They pulled up the whole "babushka" style on me, which I loved, don't get me wrong. Lots of boiled potatoes, a whole chicken, pirozhki, katleti, my grandmother even made homemade compot for me (which is juice from the fruits from our yard), they just weren't smart about it… and almost got into a fight with Larissa Kanstantinovna and we all know how that could have ended. I am fairly sure that my aunt almost put her hands on the director because she told her I cannot have bacon and kalbasa since it's not healthy. Besides, they put compot into two little beer bottles. Larissa Kanstantinovna had to sniff every bottle to make sure that it was actually juice and not beer. Talk about ghetto.

Overall, we spent about two hours together. I ate the fish and the chicken off campus, which was the only option. I was fine with that because, for a slight moment, I was in heaven with so much delicious food all at once. Are you kidding me? Yum. Yum. Yum. We spend our time mostly talking about my visits to America and my orphanage life, and I was even able to give them a tour of the orphanage. My mother barely even looked at me, which I was fine with; she can go to hell. Before they got into a car and drove off,

GOODBYES

I gave them all my pictures from America so they could see the family and hopefully forgive me for my poor life choices. I didn't have the balls to tell them that I had about two months left in this country. I didn't have the guts to break their hearts. After all of the pain that they had put me through, I didn't have the guts to do the same. So, I just stood there and waved my final goodbyes.

Maybe it's my family's visit that somehow triggered me or maybe I actually thought what would happen if I did leave this country, my home and my ancestors, the language that I had spoken my entire life. I mean I don't think I was mentally prepared until this point. Every Saturday, around dinner time, the Clays would call me to check in and see how things were going. The Saturday after my families visit, I knew exactly what I had to do. I had to tell them no... I told Masha and the other girls that I had made up my mind, and this is the final decision. Masha was the first one who laughed in my face and said that I wouldn't, that I didn't have the balls to do such a thing because why would I? Well, we all sat patiently in our bedroom and waited for the call. I sat on the edge of the bed with my right leg bouncing as my heart was pounding crazy, I couldn't breathe, but I knew this had to be done. When my phone rang, it felt like my soul had left my body. I felt useless. I answered the phone so quickly and got right into it; I knew that Oksana had to be somewhere nearby. So, I just dived right into it.

"Oksana? You here?" I obviously asked in Russian...

"Yeah?! I'm here," she said. By the tone of her voice, it was obvious that she was nervous. Maybe even as nervous as I was.

"Everything okay? Are you okay?" shit. She read my mind. I looked around the room and saw nothing but plain faces. Absolutely no emotions; if anything, it was impatient.

"Okay, hear me out. I don't want to be adopted. Before now I didn't think about my decision to come to the States and possibly leave my homeland forever. I don't think I can do this, and I am not ready. Please forgive me, and don't ever call me again." I hung up so quickly. They called right back I mean I didn't even let Oksana to say anything back; she probably didn't even process anything of what I said. They kept calling me, so I had to take off the battery on my phone. The room stood quiet, and the first one to break the silence was Masha. She looked at me with disappointment and said that I was the stupidest person she had ever met, and she walked away on me. I sat still with a smile on my face because I felt free in a sense. Because now I did not have to go anywhere far, and I could stay with my friends and be near my grandparents. I even thought about going back to them, to the village after graduating from the orphanage.

The news at the orphanage spread faster than it did between babushkas in a small village. Of course, everyone has ears, and somehow, Kevin and Aileen had contacted their people in Ukraine, who contacted Larissa Kanstantinovna… you already know I should've packed and left the second I hung up that phone call. Because the conversation that I had with Larissa Kanstantinovna and her sister Marina Kanstantinovna was too much to handle for anyone. My hair was pulled, my ears were pulled, I was pushed from side to side. I was screamed at without getting an opportunity to speak up and explain my reasoning. I mean, it was a whole circus, and I was the clown of show. Was I scared? ABSOLUTELY!!! Especially after I told them why I wanted to stay in Ukraine so I could be closer to my family. This was historically funny because both laughed, and Marina Kanstantinovna laughed a little too hard. Afterwards, she dived into giving me a lecture on how my family doesn't give two shits about me because if they did, I wouldn't be here. Maybe they were right or wrong, but my mind was already made up. Besides, I never said that I had to stay at the orphanage?? I could have easily gotten adopted into a Ukrainian family that lived close by so I could still visit my family. At this point, the news spread faster than Covid back in the day, so everyone was making fun of me and saying that leaving Ukraine and living in America was my ticket out and that if I didn't use it I would be so stupid and blah blah blah… which I already knew… I just couldn't leave my family… many would've said that I didn't have much to lose, which I would 100% disagree with. Because to me, I had everything to lose. Everything that I was within 14 years of my life. Everything that I had become within 14 years of my life. And everything that I could have been in the future.

The news of me not leaving made Denis more upset than anyone. He finally found a family who was coming to adopt him and who lived near Amherst, New Hampshire, a family who finally wanted him. He didn't make fun of me for changing my mind, but he did make me feel bad because he wouldn't have gotten through this "American dream" by himself with no one in his corner. We talked about us being adopted together and now it was finally happening,

Even though I was still in the process of getting adopted, I was still technically on the list of "poor orphan kids who need a family." This means any family could adopt me; the only difference is that it would probably be till the age of 18. After which, you get kicked out of the family because the second you turn 18, your "new" family realize that you're not the biological one, that you are an extra mouth to feed, an extra body to dress and take care of. And of course, after you turn 18 years old, the government stops paying for your expenses, so now your "new" family does not see you as a resource; they begin to see you as an orphan again. Or they never saw you as part of their family and had turned your life into Cinderella 2.0, except there was no godmother, prince, or happy ending. I knew that. I have seen it happen to girls at the orphanage, but I still wanted to give it all up and be close to my family. I knew exactly what I was risking and still wanted it badly.

Just like that, a single Mom with an older daughter showed up on the steps of my orphanage asking for a girl named Kristina… she brought at least 3 kilos of all sorts of candy, and we talked for like an hour about her family. and where they lived and what my bedroom would look like… I said yes on the spot because who gets lucky this fast? I knew that this was my chance to get out, yet I was still close by.

At this point, I was bragging that I am just one lucky soul and maybe at the end of my story, I will get what I wanted and everyone will be happy. It's crazy to think that there was someone else who wanted me?! I mean of course, it was for the money. It is always for the money. But at this moment, I just wanted to completely ignore all the red flags and move on and live. The woman who came to get to know me came again, this time with more candy and more pictures of what my bedroom would look like and she showed me what her daughter looked like and the city that soon enough would be my home. Of course, Marina Kanstantinovna did not let this slide… she and a couple of other teachers called me into their office and began to give me a lecture on pretty much how stupid I am. I tried to talk back and explain my side of the story, but no one listened. If anything, I got my hair pulled back and forth AGAIN. At this point, this lady and I were texting buddies, and occasionally, she would call me, and her daughter and I were even friends on social media. Marina Kanstantinovna told me to call her to tell her "No thanks", pretty much that the transaction is canceled.

At first, the second she picked up the call, she was, I swear, an angel, just a pure innocent woman ready to step in to be my mother. Then I told her that one of my teachers would love to speak with her to get to know her and blah blah blah. I don't want to say that it was a trap, but it seems that way now... anyways when Marina Kanstantinovna picked up that phone and also started talking, you know, normally she simply told her that the deal is off... when I tell you that that "innocent" "angle alike" turned into an angry, hungry monster really fast, I did not expect that. At this point, she was treating the whole school and how she was going to sue me and the whole school, and this is where the call got even more juicy... Marina Kanstantinovna nonworking self came out, and the swears that came out of her mouth and the other teachers and yeah, the lady was on the speaker phone, so we all, including me, heard every single word that was said out loud. The call ended with Marina Kanstantinovna threatening the woman back, saying she will break her face if she ever tried to contact me or this school again. I mean I was in shock. But really though should I be though? We knew that this lady just tried to earn the money the easy way, but holy moly, she was crazy. Marina Kanstantinovna looked at me as she gave me the phone back and said

"This is who you tried picking your mother. I saved your ass, you're welcome. Now when Saturday comes around, you better apologize to Kevin and Aileen and tell them that you are still going to America." I did not say anything. Partially because I was embarrassed, even ashamed of myself a little bit because I failed. My plan failed. And I knew I could not just call Kevin and Aileen and act like nothing happened because I knew that my words hurt them. After everything they did for me, I hurt them.

I think that, by this point, I had just accepted my faith that I had failed at everything and that my decisions had ruined my life forever. So, I just accepted the fact that I wasn't going anywhere especially with anyone, because clearly, I couldn't pick out a normal Ukrainian family who cared enough to keep me around after the age of 18. So, I told myself that I was just going to age out of the orphanage like everyone else and then hopefully go to a city college with the orphanage kids and try to live life like everyone else does. I was okay with that decision. I was okay with it because I knew I had my family near me.

It felt like everyone around me had lost faith in me, especially Denis. Denis wouldn't give up on convincing me on how this was our way out and that we aren't that lucky to get another opportunity like this. I knew that he was right, and I also knew that I could not face Aileen and Kevin after everything that I had said to them. And yes, technically, I didn't say it to their face or directly at them, but I am sure that Oksana translated and explained it all. How was I supposed to face Oksana? I felt terrible.

But in the back of my head, I was still hoping, I heard Oksana's words floating in my head. That if I wanted a change, this is the time to do it all! So, what did I do? My friends and I went to the convenience store that was a few houses down from the orphanage, and I bought the darkest shade of hair dye they possibly had. That same night, Nadia had dyed my hair in the girl's bathroom, and you already know that I had to BASICALLY hide away from Larissa Kanstantinovna… because I knew there was no way that she wasn't going to notice it and will pet me on the back of my head saying how smart this decision was. When she saw me and noticed my hair, she just sighed and shook her head at me.

GOODBYES

A couple of days later, I saw Nadia giving Masha a sticky poke on my arm in our bedroom; she used a needle people usually sew with it and pen ink. Just because Masha looked so calm and unbothered I got in line to be next. I didn't have anything meaningful that came to my head at that particular moment, and I didn't have a spot either? So, I told Nadia that I wanted a sticky poke of a musical note on the left side of my lower back. When she finished, I wanted more, I told Nadia to give me another sticky poke tattoo, but this time on the right side of my lower back, and I wanted to be the word "love." Classic. Thank goodness it's in the spot that I picked because man, oh man. If I could go back to that day, I would have at least picked a flower instead. I can't believe no one stopped me, either. Or told me that it was a 100% terrible idea. But hey! At least now it a memory.

September 1st is a national day known to be as a first day of school in Europe. At the orphanage, we have a concert to celebrate and welcome 1st graders as well as 9th and 11th graders since both of those grades are considered graduation classes. Since my class and I were going into 10th grade, we and 11th graders walked next to 1st graders. One of the 11th graders is supposed to pick up a girl from the 1st grade and carry her on his shoulder in the circle as she would ring the bell in her hand. This would show the first bell of a new official school year.

Of course, my orphanage was extra, so we would have the concert going for hours. I mean, we would have 1st graders singing and dancing and then the teachers singing and dancing and the 11th graders letting go of birds and letting off the balloons and watching them disappear in the distance. Larissa Kanstantinovna would of course give a proper and a fancy speech that would pretty much say that she was proud of us for making it this far. For many students who were not orphans and who attended the school at the orphanage because it was cheaper and better than the town schools, they would bring parents and to them, it was important seeing their kids starting school. For us, who had no one to come to support us, it was just another day. Except everyone must wear a white top and black bottoms. But this year was different. This year, I was wearing a ribbon across my shoulder that said, "Graduation class." It felt odd knowing that my classmates back at home, just a few hours away from me, were also celebrating the first day of school as well as wearing a ribbon across their shoulders that says, "Graduation Class."

Its crazy how one day could change everything. A simple 24 hours could change absolutely everything. The scary part is that the change could be good or bad right? Someone could get married within 24 hours, fall in love, or welcome a baby to this world. As well as losing someone important to you, all those things could happen within 24 hours. And to be honest, I do not think most of us humans utterly understand the power or even the consent of time. I think we all can agree that we had those days where even the seconds felt dragging, our work days? Same as school days, those last minutes before the bell goes off feel so slow. Yet, those same seconds could feel extremely fast when you miss the bus just by those few seconds. The same happens when the doctor tells you that they did everything in their power to save someone and all they needed was maybe a few more seconds of time, and chances are they would still be here with us. When we were little, all that mattered was that the sun came up, and when it came down, our day was over; it was as simple as that.

This school year was different. Different how you may ask? Well, considering the fact that my whole class did not have a classroom… my whole class consisted of four people because most of the kids graduated from the 9th grade, and here we were. Two girls and two boys trying our hardest not to laugh because what? Honestly, I am not sure how the teachers did not laugh themselves because I would think that we were wasting their time, but hey! I guess it was easier to make money this way—four students or 20, they still had to teach the same materials. But of course, no one took this seriously, and yes even the teachers who let us watch the TV during class time… honestly by this point, I was kind of upset with the universe because of course, when I started to become cool or whatever, everyone cool was gone, and were making new and cooler friends at the universities. And just like that, I was a loser ish again, but like in a cool way? Or maybe I have to disagree with that… because I was spending time together with the older students from the 11th grade? And maybe a part of me wanted those other students who graduated to see me thrive. Just maybe I wanted them to say how sorry they were to call me a boy-looking because of my hair. Just maybe I wanted them to ask me to be their friend, and just maybe deep down I wanted them to mean all of the words… but I guess in this world we cannot always get what we want.

To be honest, everything happened so fast… but when someone from the crowd calls your name and adds after, "Larissa Kanstantinovna is waiting for you," is never a good sign. This is where you pray that whatever it is you did can be forgotten and forgiven and hopefully has a solution?! Almost no one ever runs with excitement to see Larissa Kanstantinovna because, first of all, she knew all of us from head to toe, and this woman NO JOKE could recognize us by our running miles away, and second of all, Larissa Kanstantinovna had zero policy for running in the corridors so… it doesn't mean that everyone followed that policy but when I tell you that this woman KNEW she KNEW…

I remember dragging my feet as slowly as I could as I walked towards Larissa Kanstantinovna's office. I remember trying to make the small talk on the way because, deep down, I hoped she would forget it. But this woman… She deserves not only an Oscar for dealing with all of us but a whole monument! When I arrived at her office, I took a deep breath before knocking gently on her door.

"Kristina, if that's you, where have you been? You think I live here? I got papers to deal with, I got no time waiting around for you. Come on in." I mean, how could you not be terrified of this woman but at the same time do not have respect? When I came into the office, I was too ashamed of looking into her eyes because deep down, I knew that I was letting a whole bunch of people down over something that I wanted to control. For people who gave up on me a long time ago, before I even was taken away. Yeah, maybe I was selfish for doing so, but they were my family, and this was my country. And at the time, I didn't have a clue what it meant to be a Ukrainian, but I do know so now. The scary part is that she wasn't looking at me either.

(In the photo: me, the director Larissa Kanstantinovna, and Denis)

That's when I knew that I screwed up badly; it's like having your parents be so disappointed in you. Because that's who she was to us! She was a mother to over 300 children; you could say that some were better than others, but she did her best. No, let me rephrase it. Larissa Kanstantinovna did an amazing fucking job giving everyone, every single child of hers, an opportunity to do better, to see the world, to be a decent human being.

That's when she pretty much told me to get my shit together because Kevin and Aileen were on their way... to get me... I thought to myself, "wow." Because honestly, I had no idea how to be nor how to react around them after all those mean things that I'd said to them over the phone. After all the wonderful things they have done for me, I treat them like garbage. But that's when I knew it was all meant to be... They were flying across the world to get me... They were coming for me... This was the moment when I realized that they loved me, and they genuinely wanted me in their family. Because if they didn't, they wouldn't have made all this effort for a stranger that they barely knew... When Kevin and Aileen showed up, they welcomed me with open arms and gifts. Yet, before moving forward, Aileen gave me something that has been incredibly special to me till today. It was a handwritten letter from Oksana... The letter was filled with love. It was special because it was directed to me and me only. When I finished reading the letter, I smiled as tears piled up in the corners of my eyes. This was my sign that this is the right place for me to be in.

JOURNEY OF A RUNNING GIRL

(In the photo, Denis's now Father, Denis, Kevin and Aileen Clay, photo was taken at the orphanage. October 2014).

(In the photo you see Aileen Clay, Vlad, Olex, Katya, Kevin Clay, me, Lyana, Dima, and Denis. All the children in the photo were adopted into caring and loving families in the United States of America. The photo was taken in the Matveevskie orphanage cafeteria).

GOODBYES

Vlad and Olexwere were adopted into the same family in North Carolina. Vlad has been going back and forth between the two countries and is currently in Ukraine fighting for justice. Olex married and joined the Marines. Katyagot was adopted into a Ukrainian/Russian Christian family in Washington State and is now married. Lyanais is now married. Dima was adopted into a family in New Hampshire and is now working at a car dealership in Florida. Denis was adopted into a family in New Hampshire and is now living in Washington State.

(In this photo: Aileen, Kevin Clay, my now parents).

On October 10th, 2014, Dennis and I were celebrating in downtown Zaporizhzhia, celebrating the start of something new. The start of our new lives with different last names, but it wasn't just the last names that we were celebrating. We were celebrating the fact that we were no longer orphans. From that moment on, we were kids who had families, full families with parents, siblings, and even pets. (Not me though... if you see Kevin Clay, please ask him why. Denis' family had one of the cutest golden retrievers).

Even though this celebration was one of the first wonderful things someone had ever done for me, I did not feel complete. Because the second that dinner was over, the second that night would turn into a day, it meant one thing. It was time for me to say goodbye. Goodbyes to the people who made me feel at home, the people who were my friends, my family.

Kevin and Aileen threw the biggest party they could. They bought so much fruit and cake it felt countless. It was my and Denis's goodbye party. Everyone, of course, was invited, and of course, everyone showed up not because they were going to miss me so dearly but because it was free food. Not a single orphan could miss an opportunity as such. Are you kidding? But I was at the center of the attention, and I was loving every single moment of that. Kids from all sorts of grades were coming up, grabbing a piece of cake and pretending to be my friend. But I didn't care if they were pretending. I didn't care that they were eating my goodbye cake. I had about four friends sitting next to me, eating that delicious cake with the silence at our table. Not because our faces were stuffed but because we knew. We knew this was our last meal. Ever.

When Slavic's van (Slavic was the man who my parents hired for transportation purposes because they knew no matter what time it was outside or what day it was, he will get them to their destination on time if not early. He is now one of our dearest friends. And if my parents ever in the county, they have Slavic on speed dial), was pulling out of the orphanage's parking lot - I did not have a single clue of what was happening. I remember that a lot of people who were my friends and my true enemies - all came out to say their goodbyes. Without a literal thought in my head, I was giving out hugs left and right. Smiling and laughing not knowing how I would feel about this the next day, the next month, or years later. After Denis and I watched our friends waving and yelling their goodbyes, Denis and I had huge smiles on our faces because we knew that we were about to

GOODBYES

have the biggest change of our lives. That's when I heard our translator Oksana to wave back; she said:

"Aren't you not even a little bit sad? You are never coming back or will see them again." That is when I knew. I knew I messed up because there were people who I wanted to squeeze again. Squeeze as I give them the very last hug. The inside of me wanted to scream and yell "STOP THE CAR." The inside of me wanted to get out and ran as fast as I could. But I knew I couldn't do such a thing… but saying these goodbyes was one of the hardest things I have ever done. Yes of course, I had days to say my goodbyes and spend as much time as I could, but it's not the same thing as being in that moment.

(On the left: Tanya, Valya, Anna, Nicolai, and Angelina Proshak..

I begin to cry ugly and honestly, if it were any other day Denis and Dad would have easily made fun of me for crying, for being soft. Even Mom, I know this because it happens all the time at the house. But this time it was different. It was different because they all knew how much it meant to me, this place, and those people. Don't get me wrong, I hated that place. But Larissa Kanstantinovna tried her best to make it our home. Sometimes... More likely every day, I hated seeing some people; I hated my classmates because they used to make fun of me, and I hated some teachers because they would beat me. I hated it. But after everything that I have done to myself and my loved ones. Believe it or not, this was an especially important life lesson. A one-time chance to see that no one is perfect. To this day, I feel blessed that I got admitted to Matveevskie orphanage because, as I said, I learned. I learned a lot. Maybe not necessarily in the classroom but... but now I am a people person who doesn't mind sharing because sharing is caring or sharing the communal areas.

On the right, Krasovskaya Masha

As we slowly but quickly drove away, I wiped my tears away and waved my goodbyes away. Because from that moment, I realized that I had escaped.

CHAPTER 10
TIME TO GO

(Hotel in the city of Zaporizhzhia: Praga)

When I tell you we stayed at the Bujiest Hotel in the city of Zaporizhzhia... we stayed at the bujiest hotel in the city of Zaporizhzhia. Don't get me wrong, because that was my first hotel stay in the city; I have stayed in hotels before, like in America or at that time in London, when our flight left without us. But this was nice; they only had two people working there because, honestly, they weren't getting that many visitors. But they loved us! Reason one: Dad and Mom booked the rooms for about a week, so they went from having an empty house to a full one real quick. Reason two: Dad left a fat tip. With the currency exchange according to a dollar, it might not have been anything crazy, but in Ukrainian currency, it was a lot because a small hotel with maybe six bedrooms altogether turned into a breakfast-in-bed type of deal. The breakfast wasn't even fancy or anything; the ladies from the front desk would make "buterbrodi": bread, butter, and cheese with a cup of coffee. Like I said, it was not fancy at all, but it was the thought that counted. The Geiger's and the Clay's were taking over!

After we settled in the hotel, the Dads of both families went home for a couple of days to take care of their businesses. The mothers of both families had to take care of Denis and me, which does not sound like a whole lot… and for the most part, I think both of us were on our best behavior. There was one time I convinced my mom to buy me a fish, not any kind of fish but dried fish from a little kiosk down the street, and from what I remember, it did not take that much convincing because just like that, I was eating my dried fish with Denis in his hotel room as we watched a soccer game. But little did I or my mother know that the dried fish would stink up the whole hotel… and it is not a disgusting smell… to someone who has been eating the fish or grew up eating it like it is no big deal. But Denis' mom, Sue and my mom were not impressed with the smell, you could say.

Of course, we explored the city before we left Denis and I made sure that our parents tried shaurma, aka a street wrap, and yes, we did tell them that chances are high it was made with the homeless cats and dogs from the downtown streets. The look on their faces was concerned 100%, they thought we were telling the truth. The truth is that we don't even know if it was made with chicken like the menu says it was… all I know is that Denis and I ate a bomb diner that night, our parents? Not so much. But hey! At least no one got food poisoning or sick! That should tell you something, right? Of course, we also made our parents try "donner", which to be honest, I have no idea how to explain besides a giant panini looking like a huge taco. I think after seeing how it's being made, which again in the middle of nowhere at a tiny food truck - Mom and Dad have lost their appetite. We also went to a Buji Italian restaurant, it was Buji because their menu had an English option and till today, that is the restaurant that we remember having delicious food. The menu is what my parents were most impressed with. We also went to Proshak's church on Sundays and went out for a bite with them, and we went to the circus with Yana, who is my friend from the orphanage. Many memories were made before it was time to say goodbyes. All over again. Not to just people that I knew from the orphanage but the city as well.

When most of the documents were finished, we were good to go… Mom and Dad bought all four beds on the train in the room that slid with a door. But because there were only three of us…. Me and Valya had suggested that she should come with us and stay with us in Kyiv. I know it sounds crazy because she was only a teenager, but it was not that crazy because her mom Anna was coming to Kyiv for a work trip in a week anyways, and we had an extra train ticket, so if you ask me, it was perfect. It was even more perfect because Nikolai and Anna said yes! Valya and I were jumping up and down filled with happiness. The whole situation was too perfect if you ask me… and of course things went down south shortly.

We took off; at this point, the train had been moving for an hour or so. We were having a little party in our cabin, and shortly after, our party was busted by a conductor. When it was time for the conductor to check the train tickets, we were in a little "pickle", as many Americans would say.

Our fairy tale had come to an end… the conductor was very unhappy with the fact that the 4th ticket that Mom and Dad had bought did not have Valya's name on it, so technically, it was an empty ticket, and Valya herself did not have a ticket... So, what does the conductor say to us?? That Valya needs to get off the train at the next stop. All of us were freaking out, especially Valya. The only translation that my parents were getting is what Valya could put into words, I even had no idea what was happening in Russian, and to translate all that?! No thanks. So, Valya called her father. The conductor told Nikolai that my parents have to give the conductor a bribe so he could "look the other way." After Valya had translated to my Dad what the conductor wanted from us, he laughed and gave him a few American dollars. My parents were more unhappy with the fact that the conductor was willing to leave a young teenager in an unknown town all by herself than anything else.

When we arrived in Kyiv, most of our problems went away. Well, technically, I never have any problems in the first place. But it seemed like Ukraine did not want me to leave her. We needed to see all the doctors to make sure I was not bringing any diseases with me from Ukraine to America. If I remember correctly, the offices were closed, or the doctors were booked and didn't have an open appointment until weeks later. It was the beginning of October, and I don't think it was a holiday season, but for some reason, the Universe was not on our side. I remember my parents being frustrated because nothing was going their way or how they wanted, and our leave date kept pushing back. Which I? Had zero problems with. This gave us a chance to explore Kyiv and learn more about Ukrainian culture and its traditions. We got a chance to see Maidan, walk down famous street names, see big government buildings, and we even got a chance to see where our ex-president Yanukovich lived. Since he had run away, his, I shall say, mansion was open to the public as a museum; unfortunately, we didn't get a chance to see the inside of his lovely home, but the outside was plenty to get an idea of what kind of asshole he really was. We paid a little something to get in, but from what Mom said, it was nothing crazy. I mean this guy had a gold toilet seat, he had a zoo, a boat, a whole house for a guest, and so much more. After spending the entire day at this lovely museum, we didn't get a chance to see it all. We only saw half of what this guy had stolen from us...

I think my favorite memory from Kyiv is eating out at Puzata Hata. It is a traditional small restaurant that only makes traditional Ukrainian food. I am talking about borsh, any type of potato, fish, salo, and so much more. You walk around the restaurant with a trade and pick out anything you want. It is not all you can eat, which I would love, but after you put the meals on the tray, you pay for it and just enjoy it. Whenever Dad or Mom asked us where we wanted to eat, my answer always was "Puzata Hata." At some point, there was even a joke that me and Dad would open a "Puzata Hata" in America.

Photo on the left: Aileen, me, and Kevin standing in front of one of the churches in the downtown of Kyiv)

a solo picture of me in front of the same church. This is a little tradition that my parents have started. Every adapted child must get a solo shot standing in front of a monument in their home country

Finally, when the doctor's office was open for business again, we were able to do what we needed to do. I remember it was super awkward. I had to strip naked, and my now new parents were just a curtain away, like the doctors didn't even ask them to leave and wait at the door or something. I remember being super scared when the doctor saw my sticky poke tattoos from the orphanage. I was scared because I didn't want my parents to find out because I thought they would change their minds about me… You're thinking that it is impossible because who would do such a thing, but trust me, you'd be surprised. Like, I am 100% sure that if the doctor would have said that I had some type of sickness and my parents were not Kevin and Aileen and were some Ukrainian/Russian family from a small village, they would have brought me back to the orphanage. I remember BEGGING the doctor not to tell my parents about the ugly tattoos on my body, and honestly, I am not sure if that is something she could have told them, but knowing that it's Ukraine, anything is possible, especially if there is money involved. I know right, sad.

In the photo: My dearest friend, Valya and I sharing a home cooked meal in Kiev.

I remember crying because I had more goodbyes, more goodbyes to go through. Valya and Anna Proshak were also one of the hardest goodbyes because they were not just my friends that I met fighting in class over who's not going to clean up or whatever. They were family. Letting go was hard, really hard. I don't think I thought about not seeing them ever again at that moment because I was too focused on the now and not the future, but if my 14-year-old self knew that, I would have hugged them tighter.

I don't remember getting on the plane. But what I do remember is landing at the Boston MA Airport. I remember Dad telling me that the second my footsteps step on the floor of the airport, I would no longer be a Ukrainian citizen. I would officially become a citizen of the United

States of America. I remember freezing and not moving forward because going back was no longer an option; there was only one choice: moving forward and starting to live. Sounds simple right? Well, for me it was not. It felt like a big decision even though the decision itself was already made. Luckily, Dad understood how important that moment was for me, but after a minute of me just standing there of course with a huge smile on my face I had to move forward. But honestly, if it wasn't for the long line behind me, I would've stood there just a few minutes longer. After I took a deep breath and put my foot down on the ground of Boston airport, Dad gave me the biggest hug. It felt right. Comfortable.

Remember being a little sad because I was told that Oksana and the boys couldn't make it because it was a school night. I had bags and one giant suitcase, but after we got to the airport Dad asked to carry my bags and even the suitcase. I didn't know why, but when we got to the pickup area, I sprinted into Oksana's arms when my eyes found hers.

I kept picking on Dad and Mom, saying, "I can't believe you guys hide this from me." But it was a delightful surprise for sure, and guess what… They even rented a limousine to bring us home. We were that fancy. And now I was a part of that "we."

(In the photo: my now sister Oksana welcoming me at the airport minutes after I just landed)

CHAPTER 11
THE AMERICAN HIGH SCHOOL EXPERIENCE

The day we landed in America was October 31st... You already know, I was wondering what in the world was going on as we drove off and kept seeing kids not only dressed up walking around in costumes but also threatening people for candy... you could say that my first official day in America did traumatize me a little bit.

The ride home, I was feeling exhausted and super energetic and recharging at the same time. I think we all just couldn't believe this because I know I couldn't. It for sure felt like we were all together for a brief period of time, and our time together will end shortly. Everything felt the same, except it was perfect because this time I don't get to go home because now this was my home. The ride from Boston Airport was only a little over an hour long, but it felt quicker than that. My face hurt so much because I couldn't stop smiling and giggling at Oksana. There she was, my best friend in the entire world, just sitting right next to them as if no time had passed. When we arrived at the house, I just wanted to drop everything that I had in my hands and scream from the bottom of my lungs "I'M HOME." In that moment, I didn't think about anything or anyone other than myself. At that moment, everything felt right. This was the modern Cinderella story, except in this fairytale, Cinderella found her family and her home instead of some lame prince.

You should've seen my face when I walked into a bedroom, not just any bedroom but this was now MY bedroom. The orphan in me wanted to put a big poster on the door saying, "stay out" or "knock before coming in," but Dad was not 100% convinced that it was a good idea. I agree; why wouldn't I want my family to come in and to say hi? Everyone is welcome to come in!

This is so funny to me now, but that night, we ordered pizza for dinner, and guess what? I ate a salad instead because I was too grossed out by pizza, and instead, I ate a whole bowl of ONLY tomatoes and cucumbers because lettuce was different. For one we don't have this type of lettuce in Ukraine; we just normally put cabbage or just tomatoes and cucumbers in our salad. Want to hear another funny part? I ate the salad with no dressing… how embarrassing is that… I remember this so vividly because Oksana offered me ranch, and I had no idea what it was, so I tried a little bit, and I thought it was yicky. I can't believe my 14-year-old self thought ranch was gross… Dad was also laughing because he said every single Clay child that came from overseas thought the same thing about pizza; he told me it was only a matter of time before I began to eat Pizza and started liking it too. I am not going to lie; I was a little upset by the fact that not a single child came to our door to treat for candy. I was sort of ready to see it happen right in front of me. Disappointment.

Luckily for me, I didn't start school the next day that I landed. My parents thought that I would need a little moment to process the move and to adjust as well. Which I strongly appreciated that in the days that I had off before I started school, Dad and I were able to paint my new bedroom. I was able to pick any color I wanted, so I picked the color blue for the walls and yellow-colored curtains to make me feel that a part of me was still in Ukraine. To have a piece of Ukraine right there with me.

THE AMERICAN HIGH SCHOOL EXPERIENCE

In this photo: Dad and i painting my new bedroom

I didn't officially start school until a couple of weeks later, which was super nice. I started to see one of my now favorite teachers; her name was Daniella, and she was my ESOL teacher. She was teaching me English as a second language. Before I officially started school, I would see Daniella for about an hour to see where I was with the language. Luckily, she didn't run away after seeing that I was nowhere with English. All I knew was like "hi," "how are you," "good," "I love you," "bye," "cat," "dog", and probably "food." Not enough to survive by myself.

Shortly, my official first day at American High School came… November 14th, 2014, was my first day as a first-year student at Souhegan High School. In the photo, Oksana is going into her senior year and I, a tinny freshman. Except the funny part, I was not that tinny compared to my classmates at all… I mean in Ukraine, I was either an average or on a shorter side, not here. Till this day, I feel like a giraffe next to most girls.

When Oksana and I arrived at the school, I felt like I was going to throw up; all of my insides were about to come out, which would have been super cute for the first day. Am I right? I had to go to the principal office first thing when I arrived, I noticed a just as tall as me, girl was talking to the principal, shaking her head "yes" with a huge smile on her face.

Her name was Molly, since she and I had mostly the same classes every day, Molly volunteered to be my guide for the first few months, which is not what I was expecting on the first day. The school even provided me a table to use as a google translater and that's how I communicated for a few months; Molly was super nice and spending time with her all those days brought us closer. I got a chance to meet her friends get to know Molly to the point where I would call her my friend, and I even celebrated Molly's sweet 16 birthday with her friends at her house. Molly showed me around the school and introduced me to a bunch of people. But the one thing I didn't understand was the school cafeteria… if you were considered "cool" and "popular," you ate in the cafeteria, but if you were not considered "cool" and "popular," you still ate in the cafeteria, you'd just sit on the different side of the cafeteria because the front side was taken over by the cool kids. And again, if the "popular" kids chose to eat their lunch in the middle of the highway while sitting on the ground, they are fine and "cool"; however, if any other students ate in the middle of the highway while sitting on the ground they were considered "lame." Somebody, please explain…

Everyone has that one teacher whose name still comes up every other time, rather it's a conversation about high school or college. There is always that one teacher who saw something special in us, who saw something no one else did, that one teacher who checked in on you, made sure you made it to graduation day and overall didn't hate your life. His name was Steve D. It is common for a teacher to know of you if you have older siblings. Well funny enough, Steve D never taught any of my siblings, but commonly enough, he heard of our stories. From the day Steve D and I met in his English class in 10th grade, he told me that my story has a lot of potential and is truly a blessing. He made me feel I should tell my story to the entire world. He told me that a lot of people would enjoy reading my story and view my story as an inspiration. When I found out that Steve D was teaching AP classes, I felt like it was my sign to take them; I wasn't scared and wasn't nervous. During class discussions and papers, I felt seen and not judged. Sometimes, I would hold back because I was afraid of being judged by my classmates because I was still learning the language. But Steve D told me I could use it as a weapon, put it all on paper, and attack with words. In AP Comp, I realized that I actually didn't suck at writing and in fact, I enjoyed it?! After taking AP Comp with Steve D in my senior year of high school, I saw myself as a writer.

Here are some cultural shocks that I have experienced throughout my journey at Souhegan High:

- *Names.* Students called their teachers by their first names, for example, "Hey Steve, what's the homework?" you would never know if I was talking to a student or a teacher. But apparently, calling the teachers by their first name was only allowed in some schools and not all. If the first names were not allowed, then you would have to call the teachers by "Mrs" and "Ms" and add their last names at the end, which is super confusing to this day. I barely knew the difference between "bye" and "buy," and if I had to figure out if my teacher is "Miss" or "Mrs" that's so stressful

- *Dress code.* My school did not have a dress code… at all. Well, I'm assuming if you would show up naked, you'd get sent home, but it was nothing like you'd see in teen high school movies where we'd get suspended or go to detention after school. Nothing like that. I mean, we had pjs day and even the teachers would participate. You were also allowed to wear pjs to class if it wasn't a pjs day.

- *Sitting everywhere.* Everyone sat on the ground, and it was fine. I have seen this at the airport, but I thought people laid on the ground because they were tired or had to wait a long time for their flight, so what was the excuse here? Nothing. People would just eat right next to the toilet, trash cans that were just sitting also in the middle of the hallway and these weren't the cute and simple trash cans that you'd find in your bedroom. These trash cans were huge.

- *School busses.* They are 100% real, and exactly alike from the classic American teen movies. They are bright yellow giant school busses. Of course, everyone in Europe is dreaming about taking those bright giant busses at least once in their life and not going to lie I was one of those European kids who did and trust me, it's not that special. It is not like in Ukraine when I could just tell some random kid that I don't want them to sit next to me, and they'd move, one because in my school busses kids could stand up. Because we all had one school bus for the whole school, and we made it work. Five kids could sit on top of each other, or one student could have the whole row to themselves. That's just how it worked, but not here in the States. Because there were dozens of the school busses per school Buji am I right? The fun part is that when the school bus stops, the car behind the school bus has to stop at least 25 miles away from the bus, ON BOTH SIDES OF THE ROAD. And if you don't, you can get pulled over... anything for the kids, right? You were not considered "cool" if you took the bus after your sophomore year. Because at that point, you are old enough to drive, and so most kids did drove to school. But if youwere a senior who took the bus you were considered lame AF. I always thought that if the bus broke down, I could just walk home, but no, here, that would be considered weird, lame, and chances are someone would probably call the police officers to make sure that I was all right. Because people in America don't walk, they all drive. Or, of course, your friends could pick you up and drop you off, but damn, if your friends did that for you, those must be really good friends. The crazy part is that every single teenager is dying to start driving the second they turn 14.5 years old. No one drives in Ukraine, and if they do, it's not a cute Jeep or a white Mazda that their family bought them for their sweet 16th; it's probably a big minibus so they could transport people from town to town or to bring their veggies from the village to the city to sell them. Because everywhere you would go, there would be public transportation.

- *Titles for the classes.* It took me a minute to memorize each grade's titles. Because here in America, they don't say they are in 9th 10th or 11th grade. Instead, they say 9th – freshman, 10th – sophomore, 11th – junior, and 12th is a senior. This goes for both high school and college or a university. You'd just say, "I'm a freshman in college." I don't know nor understand why they choose to call themselves that, but what I do know is that it does sound fancier than just telling people that you're in 9th grade. That sounds so much lamer.

- *12th grade.* Do I even need to explain this one? In Ukraine, and I don't know about other countries, but if you're curious you're more than welcome to google this but we don't have 12th grade. Or shall I say "senior option". 11th grade is as far as it goes.
- *Snow days.* This one will always be crazy to me, but maybe not as much right now, now that I am considered a "grown adult" and it's not that I didn't appreciate snow days in high school OR college because, trust me, I did. When I first heard about my school having "snow days," I was in shock because, like I said, in Ukraine, if it snowed and the only bus for the whole school never showed up, you were expected to walk to school. And the one time the school would be expected to close down if it was on fire. And if it was, I would not be able to find out before showing up to school and finding out about it myself. Phone calls were not a thing.
- *2-hour delay.* I think my high school had this one because we just liked to be different, and I am 100% sure that most of the students, possible parents and teachers thought my high school was one of the best ones around the neighborhood. Every second Tuesday of the month we'd have a 2-hour delay for no reason provided because no matter how hot or cold it would be outside; we would still have a 2-hour delay. And those Tuesdays were golden because that was our time to shine AKA sleep in.
- *School shootings practice.* This one is and always will be a touchy subject, as it should be. Luckily, over the four years that I was at my high school, we only had one instance that involved a gun, and it got shut down quickly. One time, a freshman posted on his snapchat story a picture of him holding a gun; apparently, he got a hold of his Dad's and posted it on his story as a joke

and was never planning on bringing the gun to school or, worse, using it. The word spread fast, and when he arrived at the school, the school officer was already waiting for him. But the first time I was told to sit down and hide under my desk and not make a slight noise, I was scared. The teacher shut down the window blind and locked the door. Then, we'd hear someone walking towards us and yanking the doorknobs. This was the first time that I was scared since getting adopted and starting high school. I was a freshman. I cannot imagine that little kids had to practice this drill at an early age. No one even explained why we were doing it, because everybody knew except me.

- *School officers.* I was honestly pretty surprised to know that my high school had a police officer that was walking down the same halls as I did. And yeah, it may not seem like a bad thing for most people, but it took me a minute to cool off and not be afraid.

- *Water fountains.* The school I went to before the orphanage did not have water fountains for us to drink from. If you didn't bring water from home, oh well, what are you going to do about it? At the orphanage, however, we had two water sinks and this is where we would drink water from and get the water to wash our floors with. The water was drinkable of course, and it came from the same source. No one carried a water bottle and drank it like fish; if you were thirsty in the middle of the night you would get up, go the bathroom, and get a few sips from the sink. It was never that deep. Here??? You get judged for NOT carrying a water bottle. Because if you just walk around with a plastic water bottle, the ones from the grocery store, you'd get judged for trying to kill the planet with all the plastic. And if you did carry a water bottle, you had to make sure it's up to everyone's standards, like Hydroflask. Because in America, it's all about the brand.

- *School spirit.* My high school called this week Fang Fest week. One of the craziest moments that I have experienced while being in an American high school. When I tell you that my high school went hard, we went hard. In the first year, I didn't do as much as I did during the rest of my high school years because, duh, I had no idea what Fang Fest was until I got to experience it. Couple of weeks before the spirit week, each grade would meet with the teacher for a class discussion. During this time, we'd bring ideas on what we can be as a grade, like a theme. This is what it looked like:
  - *Monday: class colors. Freshman- green, sophomore – orange & yellow, junior – red, white, blue, and senior – black and purple.*
  - *Tuesday: any days that we as a majority had voted for, for example: 2000s day*
  - *Wednesday: the same as Tuesday, let's say pjs day*
  - *Thursday: the school colors - black and yellow*
  - *Friday: this is the craziest day of the week because this is where each grade shows up being dressed up individually on what they had decided; one year we did Las Vegas theme and my senior year we did "area 51" theme. Every grade would also decorate a specific hallway along with their theme.*

During lunch, each student who dressed up gets to vote, and at the end of the week, the winner was announced during the class assumably. But when I say my school went hard, we went hard the teachers even counted the days till it was spirit week. At the assembly, we'd play games, and each grade would show a dance that would be associated with the grade theme. Best part of the school year.

- *The school year/calendar.* I think this for sure had to be the hardest part for me to adjust to. Because in Ukraine, we follow a different calendar than here in America. So, on top of summer starting in the middle of the month summertime, people in America also trust a ground animal to decide when the winter will be over. I am also talking about the odd start times. My classes would start at 7:25am, and school would end at 2:25 P.M. But if, throughout the year, had too many snow days, they would just move the graduation date, and we continue to go to classes until we are done learning all the given material?!

- *Prom.* I don't even know how to go about this one... I'm going to start it by telling you that in my schools in Ukraine. We had one prom, and it was only for the graduation class; no dates allowed. IMAGINE THAT??! *sarcasm*. And it looked nothing like the prom in America. The whole school puts a big concert together for the graduation class, students sing and dance for them, and in the evening people celebrate. The evening celebration was obviously different at the public school and the orphanage. At the public school, families got together and the whole city celebrated, but at the orphanage, the director and the class teacher would take the graduation class to the city for dinner and a walk in the city—the end. Don't get me wrong though, an American prom should be something that everyone gets to experience at least once in their life. The dress shopping, the getting ready process, the limo, the whole Facebook prom page where the girls would post their dresses so no girls would show up in the same dress, and of course, dancing the night away at the hotel, as well as taking pictures in the middle town with your date, who's mom had to pick out the corsage for her son because he had no idea what color was your dress even though you told him many times. Lastly, don't forget about promposals. The odd part is the fact that in America, you can go to prom if you're a junior or a senior. But the fun part is that as a junior or a senior, you can bring a date who is a freshman or a sophomore or even someone from a different school. In Ukraine, prom is about celebrating you and your accomplishments. Here, it's just a dance. Many people counted their days until prom, and when that day comes, they would go all out as if it's a wedding. Which it isn't so stop spending crazy amount of money on the prom dresses that you're only going to wear ONCE.

- *The after-school activities.* The amount of after-school activities that schools provide for their students is absolutely insane. When I joined SHS, I had to choose an after-school activity myself. My options were either track or outdoor tennis, and after seeing how roughly the girls play, I chose running My school had more to offer; we had every sport in the books; we even had an after-school activity that was called "support buddy." Few students created it, and they got approved it was more of an after school social club, where a bunch of kids would hang out after school and eat chips, and it looked good on their resume. I thought running would be easy, but it was not… we had to practice every single day after school. I literally had 30 minutes to change from my school clothes into running clothes and be ready to give my all on the track. On Saturdays, we would have "going away meets" where we would meet at the school at 6 A.M. and hop on the school bus and drive for 2-3 hours, depending on where the meets would be, and this would be like an all-day thing too. Now that I'm thinking about it, I realize that this all sounds exhausting, and I'm not sure how I made it. Sophomore year of high school, I decided that I would like to dance. Every Friday, I would go to dance classes after my track practice. When I got my first job I would go to work after track practice as well. But my senior year, I chose to work full time on top of all that. This all sounds a lot, but this is very normal in America. In fact, if you don't have an after-school job or a sport that you're into, you would be called lazy. For many people, it all starts with a sport, you play whatever it is you're passionate about, many students get full rides and if you're that good and lucky, you play pro. This isn't something that we have in Ukraine, maybe we do and I just came from a poor school, but the only sports thing that we had was a class called "gym" which we do have here in America.

- *Advisory.* In the middle of our school day, after lunch, we would have a class called "advisory". A place to take a break from school and classes, a place where you could get caught up with schoolwork, this is also a place where we would chill and play board games, celebrate birthdays, and do Christmas exchange gifts for one another.

- *Free Period.* This sort of goes with "advisory," in my high school it's for seniors to have a free period. Because in your senior year, you're more likely to have most of your credits to graduate, my school would just give out free periods. If you're lucky enough, you had a free period first period, you know what that means… you get to sleep in for an extra hour or so and not come in until it's the second period. If you had the free period as your last period, you know what that means: you get to leave earlier than everyone else.

- *Leave off campus to get food.* Since I never left during my lunch to get food, I am not sure how this one worked, but I do know that some kids were allowed to leave the campus to get food during their lunch. I think parents had to sign a form saying that their child could leave the campus before you'd leave, you had to sign out in this sign-out book for students, and when you came back, you had to sign back in. Isn't that wild? Like, what if I just left and never came back? My parents would kill me lol, but I wonder if other students did that…

- *Class size.* Believe it or not, out of everything, I think this one scared me the most. In Ukraine, before the orphanage, my school had two parts to the grade; I've talked about this before, but we had 10A and 10B that's it, and both grades were about 13-15 students. After many students had left, they had to combine two grades together, so the school just had 10th grade, period, with about 15 graduates in total. At the orphanage, we also just had one grade, and it was just whatever number of students was attending at the time; my grade had about 13 of us, depending on the year haha. But when I tell you, my jaw was GLUED to the ground when someone told me that just my grade alone had like 200 kids… I was in absolute shock. And obviously, there are schools with much bigger classes in bigger states and that's just mind-blowing to me.

- *Eating in class.* This was never a thing in the schools in Ukraine or even at the orphanage, and it's not even the fact that we were poor and didn't have any snacks to bring with us because I know students who went to the school in the city and they would bring snacks for lunch and never to eat them in class. We had breaks between each class we had 5 or 20 minutes to eat if we were hungry. In America, you can whip out chips and salsa during a history class and no one will say anything; if anything, the teacher will ask for a bite. This one is my favorite. The amount of students who come to their first or second period with a cup of coffee and not homemade coffee because that's lame, but coffee from Dunkin' Donuts or Starbucks is insane. I didn't think I liked coffee until Oksana let me try some Dunks coffee where I figured out that you can ask for as many sugars as you want… omg… love at first sight. After that one moment, I became one of those people who came to their first period with a cup of iced Dunkin coffee. You already know my friend Serena and I would be on our way to Dunkin' Donuts every late start.

- *Choosing classes.* This one is also shocking to me in America, you can choose classes… I think it's great because not everyone is on the same level, and everyone has different interests, obviously, so here in America, you can meet up with your counselor to talk about classes and see what level of math you can or want to take. I liked this because it's also not all about your needs it's about your wants and that they are willing to meet you halfway to make sure you will be happy and excited about the classes you are taking.
- *Colleges.* When I tell you, the pressure is on, it's on… senior year is the easiest and the hardest year for seniors because this is the year of college essays and it's full of decisions. I think now, in 2023, many students have figured out that going to college right after graduating high school isn't the only solution to life. I know many people who took a year or two off to travel in Europe or just go out and see what else Mother Nature has for us out there, and I think that's great. Many people went to college or still go because they have to, in order to keep up their family legacy because every single family

member of theirs went to that particular college. I imagine the pressure those kids felt and probably still feel adent more school, not because you wanted to but because you were pretty much forced to? And you didn't just have to go to college; you had to pass your classes to graduate; you had to stay on top of it because if you went to college and failed or got kicked out, is the same as not going to college at all... Now, it's definitely different, and I would say now, more students decide for themselves if college is for them or not. I also think that now it's no longer about going to college to study to get a degree in whatever pays you the most money... I mean, people probably still do that, but I would say right now, the pressure is more off, and there are more opportunities for people to use their degrees or take it to the next level.

- *Bullying.* This is the one thing that I am not going to compare between the two countries to see which country bullies the most because we can all agree it's fucked up as it is. And in my 24 years of life, I am confident to say that I have seen some messed up things that people are willing to do to make someone else's life a living hell so they could feel better about themselves. I am also not afraid to say that I've been bullied myself by my family in Ukraine, by my classmates in the school before the orphanage, and of course, being bullied at the orphanage. One time, I was locked up in the classroom by two of my classmates who were, of course, boys and I am not saying that girls cannot be bullies because, if anything, I would say girls are the worst when it comes to bullying. It was their turn to clean up the classroom, and they didn't feel like it, so they locked me up and said they wouldn't open the door until the classroom was clean. And after 30 minutes of screaming and yelling, no one came. And to be honest, I am not sure if they would've left me without diner or overnight if I didn't clean, but I didn't want to find out, so I did clean. But next time, I didn't let myself be bullied. My whole life before I came to America, I was called names or people would give me not-very-nice nicknames that would just stick around for others to use. But here in America, I don't think my school has had many instances where someone was bullied. Its not like the entire world knows when someone is being bullied because with our technology, you can get bullied online which is 10 times worse. Still, there were instances that happened in other schools where many students took their lives because they felt like it was the only solution. From the bottom of my heart, I truly wish that not a single soul had to find out what bullying is.

If you ever feel alone, if you ever feel like you can't talk to anyone or considered hurting yourself in any way, please consider calling the 998 Suicide and Crisis Lifeline because help is available.

- *Graduation.* I don't want to say that graduation wasn't a massive thing in Ukraine because it is a big deal, but comparing how people celebrate "graduation day" here in America, I have no words. Students get celebrated as if they went to the moon and came back. I mean it's just high school? It's like getting an award for going to work every day, isn't it what we are supposed to do when we have a job?! I mean, for me personally, I really enjoyed the attention and the fact that people recognized my personal accomplishments because for me, it was a big deal... it was huge. I couldn't believe it. I went from being a nobody type of person to a foreigner who had graduated high school and barely spoke English. Some parents throw a giant party for their kids, invite the whole family that they have ever been related to, and they celebrate. Students even write on their cars, "JUST GRADUATED HIGH SCHOOL." Maybe it's about adulthood. Many students are between the ages of 17-19 when they graduate high school, so maybe students start being seen and seeing themselves for the first time as young adults.

- *No Public Transportation.* Even in my small, in the middle of nowhere village, I knew that every couple of hours I would be able to hop on a "marshrutka" and get places that I needed to. In the city, it would be every 15 to 20 minutes, so if you miss one, it's okay because the bus will come back shortly. Here in the States, if I was relying on a bus to get to places, I would get nowhere. I have only taken a bus a few times when I need to get to an airport on my school trip. And this bus went from point A to point B, with no stops in the middle, no nothing. Pick up – drop off, as simple as that. So, if I missed the school bus in the morning, it's not like I could rely on public transportation because it didn't even go that far into the woods where I lived. So, guess what I had to do when I missed the bus… yup, I had to wake my mother, who of course, would be very angry. Without her morning coffee and still half asleep, she would drive me to school while being angry at me because driving me to school shouldn't be her responsibility; it was my fault for poor timing. After that one time that my mother drove me to school, I never dared to miss the bus again. I like to be on the good side of my mother

- *Options at the Grocery Stores.* The number of options that grocery stores have is absolutely insane. But what else is insane is the fact that I am getting used to that, now I am being picky when I go grocery shopping. Because last summer, I tried teriyaki chips, and I absolutely fell in love with them and guess what?! Those chips were only seasonal, so now when I go grocery shopping and somehow by mistake, *wink wink* I end up being in the chip's aisle, I search with my eyes for the teriyaki chips. I don't even dare to look for any other options because I want the teriyaki chips.

Let's talk about cereal. There is a meme that everything and every flavor that ever exists at some point will be turned into cereal. You like Oreos? Try them in the cereal format. You like fruit salad? Try it in the cereal format. I'm sure at some point, Cheetos will be turned into cereal too, along with mac and cheese I mean, I am so spoiled at this point because whenever I am at a gas station, I am only looking at the new things and new flavors. And if I don't see anything, I don't buy anything, and at that point, I am just disappointed.

- *Date.* This is probably on the list of the top five things that made me angry for sure. I think at this point, America just wants to be different from everyone else, so they created this. Do you know how many looks and stares I've gotten in high school and at a doctor's office when they ask you to write today's date or your birthday and then look at what you wrote with a question mark on their face. So, you start panicking, questioning yourself if you wrote down the day of your birth correctly. 26/02/1999. Date, month, year. Of course it is correct. BUT NO, IT ISN'T. BECAUSE THERE IS NO SUCH THING AS 26TH MONTH IS THERE??? I'm sorry but let me just confuse myself and 02/26/1999.

- *American Flags & Stars.* I don't think seeing the American flag was that weird to get used to for some reason; shortly, it felt normal?! I know that many foreigners find it odd that a lot of clothing items and things in general have American flags on them. Flip flops, kitchen towels, socks, hairbrush etc., but like I said, after a while, it just became part of my experience that I adapted to quickly. I remember my first 4th of July; I wanted to wear every single item I owned with the American flag. The hat, the T-shirt, everything. The crazy part is that if you can't find anything with the American flag on it it's okay because you can mix and match with the American colors, red, white, and blue. Having GIGANTIC stars on the side of a house is what I do not understand till this day. The crazy part is when I ask what the story is or the purpose behind these huge stars on someone's house, no one seems to know. The two most common answers I've gotten from people are either they are super supportive of America like patriotic or just like it how it looks.

- *Pharmacies.* In Ukraine, a pharmacy is a pharmacy. It's a ridiculously small kiosk-looking thing where you can only buy antibiotics or health-related products. However, here in America, every pharmacy is a mini grocery store. I can go in with the purpose of only buying some medicine for a cold and come out with a case of beer, a family size m&ms, a whole bag of makeup, a teddy bear, a magazine, a pair of headphones and a pack of cigarettes and on a way out I could print some photos out from my camera roll and have my passport photo taken, AT A PHARMACY. Maybe American pharmacies are just living in the future...

- *Gaps in the bathroom.* Lol. All I have to say is that even Americans are confused about the gaps in the bathrooms. No one understands the purpose behind having giant gaps to the point where you could be sitting on a toilet and make eye contact with someone who's walking by the stall. I mean it's the oddest thing.

Also, in Ukraine, in some public restrooms like a bus station, you'd have to pay a few cents or even a 1 grivna to use the bathroom. It was very uncommon for public places to have public restrooms that you could just walk into and leave. People would just go outside behind a bush or something. When I left Ukraine, we only had one McDonalds in Zaporizhzhia, and now there are three. Fast food places like Subway and Starbucks are just being added, so it's not like you could just pull over at a Burger King to potty. You'd have to find the closest tree or a bush.

- *Eating/drinking on the go.* I think the entire world is surprised about this one. Someone once told me people in America never have time for anything, that they are always running late. That's why people go through the a drive-through of at Starbucks and drink coffee on the way to work instead of having a cup of coffee at home. Or buying the breakfast plate at McDonalds instead of having breakfast at home. The same thing as sitting down at a café to enjoy that cup of Starbucks coffee; people would just rather take it to go. Maybe people are just bad at planning their time? There were times when I saw people buy takeout at McDonald's or some Chinese food and just eat it in their car. I'm not sure if people are scared to eat in public because it's very uncommon to see someone eat out alone. But I think it's the saddest thing ever to see someone eating in their car because that's where they feel like being themselves, and that's where they feel safe.

I want to say that people abroad like to judge Americans and America overall. People say that America sucks and doesn't have any potential to get anywhere in life, as well as that people are very uneducated. Yet somehow, this is the place people can't seem to stay away from. And I got the one golden ticket because I didn't choose to come to the States. I mean, I did, but my situation was different; it was my way out. Everyone says that New York is one of the most beautiful cities and that it's the city that never sleeps - that it's the city of fashion. Of course, America is dealing with homelessness, unemployment, and unfair wages, but isn't the entire world? It is so easy to judge from the other side, isn't it? And as someone who has been living in America for 9 years, I am sure that living in Spain or Greece sounds better because one, it's Europe and two, who wouldn't want to live in Spain??? But I am 100% sure that people living in Spain or Greece have their own opinions about their homelands, which would shock us because we have no idea what is going on. Every country has two sides: the side that shows the real struggles and the side that you see on google images and that is the side that people visit and fall in love with.

CHAPTER 12
MEMORY OF THE DEAD

Sometimes, we get that one phone call that quite literally changes our lives. November 15th, 2015, I was a sophomore in high school when I got a message on a social media, "VK" from my aunt. I couldn't understand the words I was reading. As my aunt saw I was online, she called me. I stayed quiet. Numb. An uncontrollable wave of tears was coming down my cheeks. I felt powerless. Guilty. Guilty because I wasn't there to hold her hand. I feel guilty because I didn't say goodbye. Guilty because I was here and she was there… my aunt couldn't stop yelling on the other line of the phone, "SHE'S GONE KRISTINA", "DO YOU HEAR ME?", "SHE IS LITERALLY GONE", "SHE DIED AND YOU WEREN'T HERE," I think that was the first time I felt the definition of *being stabbed from the back*. I knew she was hurting, and she was right… I was not there. "YOUR GRANDMA DIED FEW HOURS AGO," it was obvious she felt alone; she didn't know what to do. I couldn't move from the couch. I was sitting here in the US while she needed me, and I was sitting here, and I couldn't do anything for her or my grandmother. I always thought she was the type of person who would never die. Who would live forever. I guess even angels have a clock…

Over forty trees were full of all sorts of fruit—apricots, cherries, pears, and apples were almost falling from those tiny branches. It was my grandfather's passion. The fruits that had already fallen from the trees were surrounded by bees, ants, and fruit flies. The smell was too good to miss. The trees were spread about six feet apart from each other, giving extra space for the future when the trees get taller and bigger. My feet were covered in dust and dirt from running around barefoot all day and watering our garden's vegetables. Waking up each morning at 5 A.M. before the sun would hit hard was necessary daily, giving us an opportunity to water as many vegetables and clean our garden as much as possible.

It was a late August evening. The mosquitoes were attacking from every angle possible – a sweatshirt was a must. The crickets were singing along, letting us know that it's almost dinner time.

My grandmother was making magic happen in the kitchen. From the distance, it was obvious that she was tired. Tired not because she didn't get enough sleep the night before but - tired. I don't remember the last time she was genuinely happy. The last time, she laughed. The last time, she and my grandfather shared a meal without arguing as if they both were just living organisms without fully experiencing what life is and, importantly, what it feels like to be happy. I wish I could remember hearing the sound of her laugh. I wish I could remember seeing the light in her eyes, seeing her eat oranges around Christmas time and hearing her say, "Oh goodness, I love Holidays!" I wish I could remember what it felt like to be in your arms, to feel your lips touch my forehead every time you wished me goodnight.

As you took your eyes off the stove, you tried to search for me:

"Kristina, come with me to the market; we need some bread," - without any questions or other thoughts, I rushed towards my grandmother, hoping I could maybe force her to buy me a chocolate bar. Money was always an issue in our family, yet I never understood why and how because my grandfather would always have money to spend on cheap locally made vodka. After a while, I stopped asking questions, finding out that my grandfather would steal my grandmother's jewelry to fulfill his wishes. As we left the house, my eyes caught four old ladies across the street, eyeing us and gossiping about our family. We heard so many people say that the devil was upon us because of my grandfather. He was an alcoholic. I knew it. Everyone knew it.

In times, whenever our neighbors needed something, my grandmother would be the first one in line to help. Whenever there was an event at our house, they would just show up uninvited and drink and eat our food. Yet, when we had no money for bread, no one reached out to help us.

"You know it's not true, right?" – my grandmother was an angel who would still try to find good in people after they would fuck her up over and over again. "They just have nothing better to do than to talk about everyone else's business," she grabbed me by hand, letting me know I am safe. People are funny in this town. They will spread rumors about you, yet the next day, they will try to be your drinking buddy.

As the sun was going down, the wind was going through my hair leaving a huge mess, almost as if the wind was trying to make me chew on my own hair. The main road was filled with deep holes, making so many cars get stuck on rainy days. No one cared enough to fix the road; at some point, the people of this town just gave up complaining because it would get them nowhere. Every house has storage dogs so they can protect the territory from outsiders. The storage dogs always scared me; I thought that they could rip their leashes off and run towards me to attack. The sidewalk was filled with dirt and old crashed fruits from the fruit trees. Whenever I would try to kick the fruits that were laying on the ground, my grandmother would say, "Stop that; it's not ladylike."

The neighborhood children were playing in their front yards in a giant pile of sand. Whenever a family has a pile of sand just lying around in their front yard, it's either because they are rich or because they were building something. The name of the store was "Nadejda," and it was named after the owner. The food market was so small that only seven-ish people could fit in at once. Tanya, the cashier, was my grandmother's friend. She would always loan us food, and we would pay her back whenever my grandparents would get their monthly pension. On a good day, she would give me free ice cream; I liked her. The market had no line, giving them an opportunity to have a small chat about pretty much everything. Meanwhile, I would wait outside, sitting on the front steps of the store.

"Kristina, you ready to go home?"

"But what about the chocolate bar?" through my voice, you could tell that I was almost begging. My grandmother slowly took her wallet out of her purse and gave me a look. I knew that look. I've seen that look before. Her wallet was empty. Our small conversation was interrupted by Tanya:

"How about some ice cream on the house?" hearing that caused a huge smile on my face, but I couldn't accept it this time. For some reason, I thought it would crush my grandmother's heart, knowing she couldn't afford it. I grabbed my grandmother's hand, letting her know it's okay, maybe next time.

"No thank you," I said politely as we left the store.

CHAPTER 13
THE COLLEGE GRADUATE

I knew from the start that I wanted to go to college. I knew that if I didn't, I would be stupid not to use this opportunity to get higher education while living in the United States of America. Deep down, there was always a thought floating in the back of my head that Kevin and Aileen would send me back if I would disappoint them enough or if they would get sick of me. So, I knew I had to take advantage of every opportunity that was presented to me. Of course, I was scared. I was actually terrified. Scared that I would also disappoint them and myself by not getting into a single college because, let's face it, I am not THAT special. There are many young adults who have a story of their own to tell. A story that would make a fine college essay. And I barely spoke English... Yet, I also knew that I would never find out for myself if I didn't try it?! You could also say that I didn't know what else was there for me if it wasn't college.

At first, I thought I could picture myself as a therapist or a person who works with child services because I wanted to help children who were struggling in their own homes. Children who were born into the wrong families, families of drug addicts or alcoholics because they didn't ask for any of it. Why should their lives be ruined by something their parents did/do? But then, I truly pictured myself as a person who would work for child services, and I began to hate myself. I remember what it felt like being taken away from my own family. Ripped off from your only blood, the only people you called "family" for the time you had walked this earth. I felt anger. I felt rage. I only saw one picture in my head, where the child services were the bad people because who does that? Who just shows up unexpectedly and takes a child away from their family?! At the time, maybe I didn't understand that it was the right thing to do, but I was a child or maybe I knew? But it doesn't cancel out the feelings stored inside me. I knew that I could not do it. I could not be responsible for making those children feel what I felt even if it meant saving their lives. When I thought I wanted to be a therapist, I wanted to go to college of Saint Rose located in Albany, New York. When I got accepted, the first thing I did was picture myself as a city girl in New York City taking a taxi to a Buji restaurant like they do in Gossip Girl. Walking on a snowy day to a coffee shop, ordering myself a large hot latte and losing track of time because I got lost in the fantasy of some romance. But things didn't quite work out for me the way I wanted them to. After I got accepted and went to the acceptance day and saw how much my yearly tuition would be, I cried. We couldn't afford it, even with scholarships too. The moment my mom and I left the financial office, I knew I couldn't do it.

I felt like I took five steps forward and ten steps backward. Suddenly, I had no idea what I wanted to do with my life; I had no idea who I wanted to learn to become, and importantly, I knew that the final decision would be mine and no one else could make this decision for me. This meant I couldn't blame it on anyone else but myself. My mother, being the person she is, wouldn't let me get upset over the insignificant things that wouldn't matter in a few years. It was one college out of millions, she said; the "one" could still be out there, but I wouldn't know if I wouldn't look for the perfect match but instead sat at home crying on my parents' sofa. That's when my mother suggested that we should start by looking at local colleges on the East Coast. Since I got adopted at the age of 14, the government considered me "independent" or whatever, which meant that some colleges were nice enough to give me free tuition. Which is pretty nice don't get me wrong, it's the college locations that worried me the most.

Mother's first suggestion was to visit the University of New England, UNH. I respectfully denied my mother's request because I knew too many people who went there, too many friendly and unfriendly individuals, I shall say. Besides, almost 70% of my graduate students try to go to UNH. No thanks. Besides, the number of times I used to get lost at that school trying to look for a bathroom when I did track and field when we had a going away meet at UNH are too many to count. When my mother suggested Keene State College, located in the small town of Keene NH, I had nothing bad to say. I have never been to Keene; even though a suitable number of students from Souhegan High tried to go there, I did not have anything else to say. So, one lovely, rainy Saturday day, my mother and I decided to tour it and give it a shot; it wouldn't hurt, I thought. I knew that going to New York was not an option anymore, so I had no other option but to try and give my best judgement to these schools. Even though it was a rainy day, that did not bother me at all because the second I put my foot on that campus, I absolutely fell in love. Which I didn't think it was possible.

All it took was to glance through some windows and see students sitting at a table typing away. A person who knew how to use his words and the right words. And just like that, I was absolutely amazed. From that one visit, I immediately saw myself as one of those students sitting during a two-hour class taking notes. I wanted to scream, "This is the one!" from the top of my lungs.

(August 2018, Dad, and I wearing all the Keene gear)

Just like you see in the movies about college, I got myself in some questionable situations that made my family and I question myself. The smell of freedom was too good to miss, just like the smell of fresh muffins coming from the kitchen. I went from having over 3.0 GPA to an average of 2.0 GPA just in my first year. I also managed to get on a year-round probation with the college for underage drinking. I had to attend AA meetings 3 times per college requirement. At these meetings, I saw familiar faces that I had met at parties and even college dorms and classes. We would exchange some smirks and even giggle every now and then. It was pretty funny until the head RA had a one-on-one meeting with me, informing me that around Thanksgiving break, my parents would receive a letter from the college stating that I am on probation. My heart sank. I begged and begged not to send that letter because I was 19 years old and considered an "adult", but it didn't matter how old I was; I was still underage. The image of my parents' faces kept blinking right in front of me. I couldn't even imagine the disappointment.

It wasn't until my mother pulled me aside and said, "Do you really want to be like your mother?!" Those words were like a sharp blade that went through my heart. I couldn't believe what I heard. Besides the feeling of being hurt, it was a moment of awakening. A moment of realization. I had to find my purpose and finish what I only dreamed about – graduating from college and having a higher degree.

The summer before my sophomore year, I realized that I was $1,000 short... even though I was getting free tuition and my college loans were covering most of the expenses, I still had to pay out of pocket for the two semesters of my freshman year, I had the scholarship to cover those "out of pocket" expenses. Unfortunately, I spent that money on what I thought was more important at the time, it was too late to do anything about that. When I came to my father to propose a plan where he would lend me the money, and I would pay him back the second I got a job. He was still deeply disappointed in me; he gave me a chance to give him the speech, but when it was his turn to speak, he's speech was a lot shorter... it was a simple "Tina, no." Another knife in the back... when I asked him "why," he said that he didn't believe that my head was truly in it, that I wasn't "worth the investment" and maybe "if you're struggling, maybe you need to take a gap year and find a job so you can pay for it." I told my father that if I take a gap year, I wouldn't come back to school, which didn't seem to change his mind. As I left my parents' house, the only thing that I was thinking about was that I wasn't "worth the investment." I spent hours breaking down word by word to figure out what exactly he meant and what his words meant to me personally. I couldn't quite figure it out, but what I knew is that his words hurt me. But I also knew that I made him feel that way about me. The choice I made disappointed him. He couldn't have said those words for funzies. He saw right through me. He knew I wasn't ready. And the reason why I was in this situation was no one else's fault but mine. My older brother Sergey ended up selling his motorcycle behind my back to make sure I had the money to go back to college. He said that he wanted to see me graduate college; he wanted to be there to see me walk across that stage and get my diploma, that I should finish what I started.

Fly High Brother, 03/19/1998 - 09/12/2021

Being a college student is everything you see in the classic American movies and teen shows. It's all about partying and who can shotgun a beer the fastest without throwing up.

Of course, after living with the Clay family and coming to college, I felt like a caged animal finally getting a gasp of freedom. There were no longer house rules on what time I should be at home and what time I should go to bed; the "no sleeping past noon" was out of the window, as well as eating healthy. Dominos should've sponsored my roommate and I for all the late-night orders we had placed. Half of my tuition must have gotten to Dominos. Balance. After I turned 21, I had found myself thriving and trying to do better. I wanted to do better for myself and prove others wrong. I wanted to graduate college and be able to hang my college diploma on the wall. Living off campus made me get out of bed and go to work. This is where I was able to find that student balance. I continued to pay for college myself after taking out a loan from the school. You can still be a college student and enjoy a night out legally, too. Just like that, I was able to get my GPA up and be on the honor list for junior and senior year. I was noticing a difference. At this point, I knew I could do it, and I wanted my parents to know that I could too.

Sometimes, what you think is the "hardest" goal or an accomplishment is easier than what is happening in your environment. Let me break that down for you. My whole life, I have been sharing everything. It wasn't until the Clay family adopted me that I had my own bed, and I was not even talking about the bedroom overall. Before the orphanage, I had shared the meals with my grandparents. The last bite of the bread shared the place where I was sleeping; at the orphanage, it was rare that you had something of YOURS, and it was YOURS only. We shared a bedroom, bathroom treats, clothes, and everything else. It was fine. It taught me a lesson about sharing, even if it's the last thing you have.

Living off campus was fine. Sharing an apartment off campus with three other girls was also fine. Until it wasn't. I have never had anything against not only girls but anyone borrowing something or using something of mine. If anything, it has always made me feel wanted and good. Like, wow I have something you like or want – yes please. Have it. It is one thing to mention it sometimes "Tina I had borrowed some of your X" and it is another thing to use it and share it with the entire world and never mention it to me. Scenario: my boyfriend's parents had gifted us a fancy (I am talking high class) giant bottle of maple soup. We had no problem sharing it with all my roommates. At this point, we might have used it once or twice, right?! One lovely day, one of my roommates invited a bunch of girls for brunch at our apartment. Did she tell any of her roommates that she had people coming over? No. Did she use most of our groceries for mimosas and pancakes? Yes. Did she clean up after herself? No. Did she put an empty bottle of maple soup in the fridge for me to find weeks later? Yes.

I would love to say that I have seen it all?! And I can already see my father, Kevin Clay saying something as "Just wait till you live as long as I have, you'll see some interesting stuff". (No offense Dad, love you). But I have. I have seen it, maybe not here in the United States but mostly. I have not only seen it, but I have also lived through it. I took part in IT.

Outside of it all, I am a girl who now has her college diploma hanging on the wall of her bedroom. I am now a girl who has a full-time job doing what I love, and importantly, it has NOTHING to do with my degree in English, but who is using their degree nowadays??! I am just a girl who is doing okay in life and who is happy (depending on the day), but we are all allowed to have a bad day.

To answer some of y'all's questions. I periodically speak with my aunt and Olga on the phone; life had a different path for both of them, and it's terribly sad to see them both in such a position where none of them have control over their lives. My aunt Inna had bought a house next door to

THE COLLEGE GRADUATE

my grandparents' house. In the house, an elder Grandma, Nina, used to live, the one whose garden I used to steal vegetables from. She had died a few years back, and her daughter from the city sold the house to my aunt. Which at the time seemed to be a good idea because she was my grandfather's eyes.

I am not sure at what age in your life you become to think less of yourself, but it is very clear to me, my aunts' neighbors, and the whole town that this stage in her life came sooner than it should have. My aunt is in her 40s, and if she had access to the medicine that she needs, she would have been thriving. I know that her life has been a rough patch, and I wouldn't want to wish her life onto anyone I know. She constantly blames herself for not being able to find a husband and not being married. She constantly blames herself for not being able to have children. But those things are way out of her control, and I wish she would see herself the way I have seen her. I mean we had our rough moments because she is my aunt, but for the most part she's been a great friend to me, besides of course being a role model and of course, a mother figure in her own way. Somehow, my aunt met this guy named Sergey who's in his late twenties beginning thirties and thought he got it "good." My aunt collects some type of disability for her eyes and not being able to see, and I am sure that its barely anything, especially considering what is going on in Ukraine right now; every little cent matters. Since my aunt can barely see, she always sends Sergey to the store to go grocery shopping and buy the necessities that you would need to live on.

Anyways, one day she gave Sergey the last money that she had, and Sergey KNEW that it was all they had. Guess what he did???? He never showed up. Well, let me rephrase it… he showed up a week later, drunk, CRAWLING on his knees yelling for forgiveness, and he was not only drunk, he also showed up with a new phone. I mean, when I heard about this…saying angry is being genuine. I have met Sergey once when I FaceTimed my aunt. I specifically asked to meet him because I needed to know what was so special she was seeing in him. Nothing. Nada. Nechego. Absolutely nothing special was seen in this man, who is pretty much my age. What I did see was that he was an asshole who is using this situation left and right. And I had talked to my aunt about his attitude and his choices and actions because this cannot be beneficial to her; if anything, he is going to get her bankrupt and make her even more embarrassed than I am sure he already has. When I was talking to him on the phone, he was laughing at what I had to say; he was just shaking his head at me, and I mean, it was obvious that I knew all about his little adventures around town because, let's be honest I do have eyes and ears but I have realistically connections there. All it can take sometimes is a little bit of manners?! But I could tell that my aunt was uncomfortable by the fact that I was yelling at him as if he was her little kid and I was the teacher putting him in his place, but that is how it was?!

At some point, he just got up and left from the camera. The truth hurts my guy. The scary part is that my aunt whispered to the phone after Sergey had left the screen and I was no longer able to see him and said, "Kristina stop. We have to go but I will call you later." I was scared for her. I didn't know what to do or what to think. Why couldn't she just say that aloud. Why did she whisper?! The first thing that just came to my mind was that he was putting his hands onto her. And yes, it was floating in my mind, but I was holding onto the bad-ass memories I have of my aunt. I mean, why couldn't she just beat him up or put him in his place? That was my first thought. There was absolutely no way that the same woman who took on some mountains, who broke into houses, who dated criminals, the badass aunt who chased people with the knife when she was looking for me, and now this same aunt is receiving punches left and right??? How is that fair? I understand that you can't stay the same person, and her body is different now, but she couldn't just give up on herself and just take it all like that. I won't let her. When I found out that he was hitting her, I felt more rage than ever, but what could I do with all of what I was feeling? Absolutely nothing from all the kilometers in between us. I didn't just sit still, I will tell you that.

You already know how in small towns, everyone knows each other and each other's business whether they want to or not. The town's newest addition to the police crew is a friend of mine who used to go to the same school as me. Luckily for me, we kept a good enough relationship, and I had no problem reaching out and asking for help. I asked Sashu to investigate him and provide more information on who this individual Sergey is. Sasha didn't even have to take time to figure out who I was talking about because he knew right away, and let me tell you… he did not have the nicest things to say about him. You could pretty much say that I was right about him and his shitty personality all along. Sergey is the type of guy who is constantly looking for trouble and an enjoyable time. No matter who it is with or who it will affect because clearly, he has nothing to lose except my aunt, who I truly hope will soon come to her senses; I know she hasn't yet, but I would pay so much money to see her drop Sergey and just let her be or find someone who truly deserves her love.

My aunt took care of my grandfather and was there for him when he was lonely. But I guess his lonely days were not that lonely because one of his mistresses pretty much moved in ish when she found out that my grandmother had passed away. I guess she is a businessperson in her village a few hours away who owns a few farms and is rich. Once she heard the news that my grandfather is "lonely" and is drinking his sadness away she had realized that she still loves him. She had asked my grandfather to move in with her, and honestly??? If he had said yes to her and had left that sad place filled with disgusting memories behind, I would not have been upset a bit. But he told her no. My aunt told me that my grandfather missed my grandmother every single day. Every single day and every single sip of alcohol that would enter his body, he was thinking about my grandmother. My grandfather would speak highly of his wife. In my opinion, he had ruined her life for absolutely no fucking reason. I am angry. I am angry that God or Mother Nature has a book or a timeline for people. I am angry that she was gone first. I am angry that the earth had allowed him to walk more, giving him more days to live. Yes, I understand and is happy that he was speaking of my grandmother highly and that he had FINALLY realized that their marriage wasn't happy or perfect and that he was a narcissist. Makes me actually want to think that he possibly loved her. In his own messed up way… But why? Why does it take someone's death for that person to be highly spoken of? Why does it take someone's death to be loved in the first place?!

When my grandfather didn't say yes to his secret mistress, I, unfortunately, don't know her name; she didn't stop her visitations. Even though he had told her that he didn't want anything to do with her, she didn't stop showing up. Sometimes, she just had to make sure he had food and clean sheets. Months before he had passed away, he was diagnosed with schizophrenia. No one knew he was sick or what he had until it was too late. But months before his death, he would forget about doing simple tasks with the people he loved. One day, my aunt came over to bring my grandfather some soup, and he asked her if she had any cigarettes. They ended up smoking a cigarette and even had a full-on conversation. A few minutes later, he asked my aunt if she had any cigarettes on her and if they could smoke, to which her reaction was concern and confusion since they had just smoked one. When

THE COLLEGE GRADUATE

she mentioned that, my grandfather completely freaked out and grabbed what was the closest to him, in his case, a glass plate, and he tossed it at her face. As he threw that plate, he was screaming at my aunt, saying, "Who are you?" and "What are you doing in my house?" The plate that he threw at my aunt broke and ended up causing a bleed and slicing some of her skin off on her face. She didn't have the money to get the stitches done by the doctor, so her new 25-year-old boyfriend helped her. Now you can imagine what kind of materials they had and what those stitches looked like.

After I had FaceTimed my aunt, I could tell you that her scar didn't heal very properly… later on, my grandfather was all over my aunt's business, asking her who had done that to her face. She wasn't sure if she should tell him the truth, not knowing how it would affect his mental state. When he heard what he did to his own daughter, he couldn't believe himself. But an apology can only do so much. My aunt was not upset with him; I know she could never be. And I think deep down she also knew that he wouldn't just toss a plate at her face, that something was going on. Unless of course, he was drunk out of his mind. After seeing that he was acting like himself, everyone assumed that whatever the incident was, it would never happen again until it did. The incident did happen again. Except this time, my aunt had to call the doctor to come get my grandfather. When the ambulance came to his house, they took him to the hospital. My aunt and my mother happen to be together, which I guess is a rare occasion. My aunt stated that after they brought my grandfather to the hospital, after a while, he was doing okay. They had to pump his stomach, and they knew he was doing okay because he wouldn't stop yelling at the poor nurse who was just trying to do her job. When my grandfather realized that he was at a hospital, he wanted to go home right away, which, to be honest, is a fair reaction. Unfortunately, on the day of January 20th of 2023 - something happened, and the doctors had to perform an operation; my grandfather died on the operation table.

"Dear Grandfather, Dedushka, Vladimir, Vovachka, Vova

As a young girl you were my hero. You were my leader who I followed and who I wanted to look up to. In school, when I had to write about my "idol" when many chose to write about singers and astronauts, I chose to write about YOU. Yet around the age 5 or 6, I started to realize that you weren't my idol anymore and I wasn't your little princess anymore because you began to see HER in me. My actions began to remind you of HER. I was her doubleganger, and you hated every moment of it. Yet, I didn't start hating you because your special love for me has cooled off overtime. My love started to cool off for you when I began to see who you really were. A psychopath. A liar. An abuser. A hater. A selfish human being. With time, I wished to be not related to you because each time I saw you hit Grandma - every nerve inside my body would boil, and deep down, I wished to do the same to you because you were the most judgmental person I've known all my life. And when you began to raise your hand on me, you were a nobody to me if anything, I was ashamed to know that just few years ago, I saw you as an idol and, worse wanted to call you "father". And thank God for Grandma not letting me because I would rather be fatherless and starve than have call you Dad.

You had 3 kids yourself, and where are they now? One died almost in your arms because you weren't there to teach your son how to swim. Because at the time, you even bought off your kids. You thought a few gold essentials would buy you the Dad of the Year award. Your young daughter? Oh yeah, the one that carries the title of my mother. Makes you gag every time she walks into the room, but why? Because she's a whore. Because she sleeps with old man for money as if its her fault. Or is it because me, Mom and Grandma all look alike, and you just cannot stand that? Well, how did she get to this point? Have you ever asked yourself? Maybe you're the reason why all of your kids are so fucked up. Your older daughter? You mean the one who you treated like your buddy and not your daughter? The one who would have taken cities and countries if you simply asked? Or did you hate her because she was a copy of you? Well, I guess not all of us are perfect, are we? I bet you never had a single thought float in your brain "is it me". Because maybe it was all your fault. You were supposed to be our super glue; were you supposed to be the head of the family instead? You were the alcoholic of the family who sent most of his family away. I don't even remember the last words that I've told you.

I don't care, though, and maybe a few years from now, I will regret all the things that I've said to you in this letter since you never let me speak. And maybe even I'll forgive you, but right now? Right this fucking moment, I hate you. You're gone, and I am still here. And maybe you were in a living hell your last days, and maybe I am a little sorry for not holding your hand to say the final goodbye or seeing you one last time, but you're gone, which means your pain and your suffering are gone too. And I still get to live with the scars on my body that YOU had left for me. That YOU had left on MY body to see and remember each day. I still get to go to bed and wake up remembering each time you had hit me. Each time, you made me feel bad about myself because I looked like HER. My mother. Your daughter. How was that my fault? I did not deserve half the shit that YOU alone had put me through. Now that you are gone, Inna gets to cry every time she looks next door at your house. Even though you had forgotten about her the past years, she's not okay either because she needed her father, and instead, she had to wipe some drunk's ass. I am so fucking angry about the fact that you left without knowing how I feel, without knowing that I know, that I remember.

Rest In Peace Grandfather."

You know. I know. I am THE girl they talk about back in my small village. Because I am one of the million little children who was stealing, breaking into stores and houses and who is thriving now. They might be saying that I didn't deserve this chance and should've died by now and be buried right next to my family OR they might be saying that I am one lucky girl who got away from my family. But I am thankful to both. I am thankful for being alive, and I will always be thankful forever for the fact that Kevin and Aileen Clay saw something special in me and believed that one day I could be someone when no one else did.

What now you may ask?! I finally know who I am. I am a young woman. I am a college graduate. I am a sister to 8 siblings. I am a daughter. I am a girlfriend, and one day I will become a wife. I am a girl who loves sunsets and sunrises and the girl who loves her cats. Although, I will also be an orphan at heart. At heart, I will always be a Ukrainian girl whose biological mother didn't want anything to do with her. At heart, I will always be a Ukrainian girl from a small village whose grandparents tried to raise her but couldn't do so because of their alcohol problem. I will always be that girl who ran away from home. Yet, that does not matter. Because now, all those things, the good and the bad, make me who I am today. An individual. An individual with life purpose but, most importantly, an individual who matters. I matter, and so do you.

EPILOGUE:

What if I told you that once in a little while, I get this awakening moment that makes me stop what I'm doing and remember. Remember it all. The abuse. The cries. The long, lonely nights spent outside. It hits me like a brick falling from a tall building in New York City and I remember. Remember it all. Hungry. I remember my stomach eating itself because that was all I had. I remember being who I was while growing up. A thief. An ugly human being breaking into markets fighting for life to stop hunger. Stealing from elderly people because I was the victim, or was I? I remember being lonely. Talking to myself aloud, asking if that's all I ever will be. Asking the universe why me? Why is it me who was born into this family? Why couldn't I be born into that girl's house who lived just a few houses down the street from me? I also remember the memories.

I remember every single tree that was planted in my grandfather's yard. I remember the romantic movie nights that I watched with my grandmother. Crying, laughing and eating sunflower seeds all at once. I remember going back to school shopping, I remember the delicious breakfasts she made me in the morning. I remember her holding my hand every doctor visit or every time I fell onto ice and had to run home because I couldn't feel my hands and she would blow her love and warm me up. I remember the night she stayed up checking in on me because I was sick. I remember her snuggles being so tight I remember her playing with my ear to help me fall asleep. I remember it all, and I miss it. Would that make me selfish? Of course, if I had a Time Machine, I would go back in time and stand up to my grandfather.

I don't miss the abuse, or spending nights in the doghouse outside or being hungry. I miss being home.

If I could see my grandfather right now, I would sit him down and make him remember. Make him remember all that he did to me, my grandmother and even his daughters. I would want him to remember it all! Do you think he forgot? Do you think he ever cared? Even a little? I would want him to know that I remember it all once in a little while.

And when I am done being sad and that moment that reminder goes away, I tell myself three things before moving on with my day. I have a bed. A bed that I get to call mine, a bed that is comfortable. A bed that I get to crawl into after an exhausting day at work. I have four walls. Four walls that surround me and protect me from the outside world if there's danger or as simple as the weather. Four walls that keep me safe and warm and that I get to call home. I have food on the table. Food that fills up my stomach. Where at any moment I can freely get a snack. I am blessed. I am lucky. I am rich in life.

ACKNOWLEGEMENTS

There are countless people who have been part of this journey, who I am forever grateful for.

First, I thank God for blessing me with strength when I had none.

To my adoptive parents, Kevin and Aileen Clay—Mom and Dad—thank you for choosing me, for believing in me, and for giving me the gift of a complete family. Your love, support, and faith in me have helped me be the person I am today.

To my siblings—Alec, Vovka, Anya, Oksana, Sergey, Nick, Tanya, and Kolya—thank you for welcoming me into your lives. For the laughter, memories, and unbreakable bond we share – I am grateful.

To my High School English teachers—Jen Spara, Steve Dreher, Melissa Ann, and Daniela Loose—thank you for seeing my potential, for believing in me when I struggled to find the right words – for never laughing at me when my English was broken. Your encouragement gave me the confidence to tell my story and to put myself out there.

To my dearest friend Serena—thank you for always being there to listen; for sitting through endless read-aloud sessions, and for helping me make sure every word sounded right and every sentence made sense. Your patience with me and support has meant more than I can express.

To all of the people who are still fighting for hope—this story is for you.

And to the reader, thank you for walking this path with me.

"Your present circumstances don't determine where you can go; they merely determine where you start."
—Nido Qubein

www.ingramcontent.com/pod-product-compliance
Lightning Source LLC
Chambersburg PA
CBHW032108090426
42743CB00007B/284